Puppet Scripts for Use at Church

No. 2

Puppet Scripts for Use at Church

No. 2

Everett Robertson, Editor

Broadman Press
Nashville, Tennessee

© Copyright 1980 • Broadman Press.

All rights reserved.

4275-19

ISBN: 0-8054-7519-2

Dewey Decimal Classification: 812.08

Subject heading: PUPPETS AND PUPPET PLAYS

Library of Congress Catalog Card Number: 78-72843

Printed in the United States of America

Introduction

Puppetry continues to grow as an exciting communication tool in the ministry of the church. Everywhere churches are discovering the ability of the puppet to break through communication barriers constructed by an increasingly alienated society.

These delightful inanimate objects that take on human characteristics have an almost unlimited ability to successfully communicate information. They are particularly successful with getting across information that is not transmitted through more traditional church communication processes.

This book directly supports *Using Puppetry in the Church* (Broadman Press). This collection is aimed at partially filling the need for puppet scripts. The scripts in this book vary greatly in style, form, and subject matter. Many of the scripts can be outlines for other scripts that puppeteers can write to fit the needs of their particular ministry.

The book has been conceived with the intent of relating to all ages. Children's workers in particular will need to take care in selecting scripts. Consider subject matter and language when making such selections. Also, when using puppets, follow guidelines presented in major Children's leadership materials.

Five major areas are presented: Promotion, Bible Study, Seasonal, General, and Fun and Fellowship. The fun and fellowship section is small because many scripts in other sections may also be used here. The promotion section has several scripts that are general in subject matter, so they can be used to promote anything. Simply fill in the blanks with the activity being promoted.

The Table of Contents places each script under an appropriate heading. Some script listings include a word or phrase in parentheses. This describes the subject matter of the script if the title is not definitive. Also included is the number of puppets necessary for producing each script.

For additional information on puppet books or puppets, contact Broadman Press or The Church Recreation Department, 127 Ninth Ave., North, Nashville, Tn. 37234.

Contents

Section I: Promotion

What's Happening? (3 puppets) 10
A Winner (5 or more puppets) 10
The Best Storybook (Bible Study) (4 puppets) 12
God's Road Map (Bible Study) (Ventriloquist, dummy) 12
The Library (Bible Study) (2 puppets) 13
Johnnie's Suitcase (Bible Study) (2 puppets) 14
Do You Go to Church? (Attendance) (5 puppets) 15
Witnessing? (2 or more puppets) 16
Fishers of Men (Witnessing) (2 puppets) 16
Be Prepared (Witnessing) (2 puppets) 17
Stewardship (5 puppets) 18
Diggin' Deeper (Stewardship) (2 puppets) 18
Stewardship (3 puppets) 19
Something Special (Fund Raising) (Pastor, 3 puppets) 20
I Like Me (Promotes Puppets) (2 puppets) 21

Section II: Bible Study

What a Day (Ps. 118:24) (2 puppets) 24
Somebody's Watching (Ps. 118:24) (Narrator, 1 puppet) 24
Sonlight (Matt. 5:16) (1 puppet) 25
Working Together (Evangelistic) (2 puppets) 26
Face Your Problems (Phil. 4:13) (2 puppets) 26
Nothing Is Impossible (Luke 18:27) (2 puppets) 27
Covet? What's That? (Ex. 20:17) (2 puppets) 28
The Big Test (Love Your Enemies) (2 puppets) 29
School Blues (2 Tim. 2:15) (2 puppets) 30
And the Winner Is . . . (Matt. 6:19-21) (2 puppets) 31
Samson—a Man-Sized Thirst (4 puppets) 31
Let's Be Friendly (Zaccheus) (Ventriloquist, dummy) 32
Noah's Ark (2 puppets) 33
Incident Near a Snake Farm (Moses' Brass Snake) (3 puppets) 34
The Rebelling Son (Prodigal Son) (6 puppets) 35
How to Be a Witness Without Being Weird (Good Samaritan) (6 puppets) ... 36
When I Am Afraid (David as a Shepherd) (3 puppets) 37
Harry the Skeptic (Jonah) (Pastor, 1 puppet) 38
Penelope Prays (Pharisee and Publican) (2 puppets) 39
If You Ask in Faith (Matt. 21—22) (3 puppets) 40

Section III: Seasonal

A Christmas Experience (1 puppet) 44
'Tis the Season to Be . . . (at least 5 puppets) 44
Christmas Joy (4 puppets) 45
Sharing with Others (Christmas) (2 puppets) 46
Incident at the Christmas Tree Lot (3 puppets) 47
A Christmas Card from the Puppets (Narrator, 4 puppets) 48
The Greatest of All Christmas Gifts (Voice, 4 puppets) 49
The Christmas Spirit (3 puppets) 51
Puppy Love (Valentine's Day) (2 puppets) 53

Play for Puppets Who Forgot to Practice (5 puppets) 53
America, My Country (Fourth of July) (3 puppets) 54
Oh Yes, Thank You (Thanksgiving) (4 puppets) 55
Thanksgiving (2 puppets) 56

Section IV: General

All Aboard for Heaven! (Evangelistic) (6 puppets) 60
Wages of Sin (Evangelistic) (3 puppets) 61
A Saved Sinner (Evangelistic) (1 person, 2 puppets) 61
Is Jesus Inside of You? (Evangelistic) (2 puppets) 62
Boeing's Concept of God (Evangelistic) (1 person, 1 marionette) 62
Jesus Taught About God's Love (Evangelistic) (2 puppets) 63
Where's It At? (Evangelistic) (3 puppets) 64
Good Ole Teacher (Evangelistic) (Ventriloquist, dummy) 65
Don't Interrupt Me, I'm Praying (Prayer) (4 puppets) 65
Yes, No, and Wait and See (Answered Prayer) (2 puppets) 66
The Puppet (All Things Are Possible Through Christ) (1 person, 1 puppet) .. 67
Incident at the Grand Canyon (Witnessing) (Voice, 2 puppets) 68
It's Love (Witnessing) (2 puppets) 69
The First Youth Choir Tour (Witnessing) (4 puppets) 69
I Miss My Grandmother (Witnessing) (2 puppets) 71
A Friend Is a Gift You Give Yourself (2 puppets) 72
The Brick Wall (Friendship) (Narrator, 2 puppets) 73
Let's Be Honest (Friendship) (2 puppets) 73
I Need You Too (Friendship) (3 puppets) 74
The Math Problem (Forgiveness—Matt. 18:21-22) (2 puppets) 75
The Turned-Over Wagon (Forgiveness) (1 person, 3 or more puppets) 75
Once a Frog (Forgiveness) (2 persons, 1 puppet) 76
Looking at a Christian (The Christian Life) (3 puppets) 77
Share Your Soda? (Sharing) (3 puppets) 78
The Backstabber's Suite (Gossip) (6 or more puppets) 79
You Don't Say (Gossip) (2 puppets) 80
I Love Me (Self-Centered) (2 puppets) 81
Me First (Self-Centered) (5 puppets) 81
How's Your Love-Self? (Self-Respect) (6 puppets) 82
God Made Me Special (Discovering Ability) (2 puppets) 83
No Longer a Schmeil (Spiritual Gifts) (3 puppets) 84
Post-Basketball Game (Discovering Ability) (3 puppets) 86
Mowers and Frogs (Discipline) (4 puppets) 87
The Lost Book (Responsible Actions) (2 puppets) 88
King of the Jungle (Leadership) (Narrator, 3 puppets) 89
Why Are People Different Colors? (1 person, 1 puppet) 89
Keeping God's World Beautiful (Ecology) (4 puppets) 90
Hi, God! (Thankfulness) (1 puppet) 92

Section V: Fun and Fellowship

A Bible Lesson from the School of Hard Knocks
(2 Voices, Narrator, 3 puppets) 94
Incident During a Visitation Campaign (Narrator, 2 puppets) 95

Section I

PROMOTION

What's Happening

by Greg George

Henry: Hey, Fred, did you hear what's happening _____ (date)?
Fred: No, what's happening?
Henry (*Surprised*): You mean you really don't know what's happening _____ (date)?
Fred: No, I really don't! So what's happening?
Henry: You haven't seen any of the posters about it?
Fred: About what?
Henry: You haven't received a letter with the details about it?
Fred: No, about what?
Henry: No one has telephoned you with the information either?
Fred: No, they haven't. Now will you please tell me what is happening _____ (date)?
Henry: Now you're sure you haven't seen any of the buttons?
Fred (*Louder*): No, I haven't seen any of the buttons.
Henry: And you haven't noticed any of the bumper stickers?
Fred (*Louder*): Would you please stop and tell me what is going to be happening _____ (date) before I get mad?
Henry: OK, OK, so you don't have to get all excited.
Fred (*Apologetic*): All right, I'm sorry I got mad.
Henry: I mean, we are the best of friends.
Fred: I know, I know.
Henry: I mean if you wanted to know what's happening _____ (date), all you had to do was ask.

Fred (*Very calm and cool*): Let's just start all over from the beginning, all right?
Henry: Sure, that's fine with me.
Fred: Good! Now you walk up and ask exactly the same question you asked a while ago. All right, go.
Henry: Hi, Fred, did you hear what's happening _____ (date)?
Fred: No, Henry, I didn't hear; what is happening _____ (date)?
Henry (*Playfully*): You mean you really don't know?
Fred (*Loudest*): HENRY!!!!!
Henry: I was just kidding; I was just kidding. On _____ (date) we're _____ (event), but I guess everybody knows by now. See you later, Fred. (**Henry** exits. *Enter* **Herman.**)
Herman: Hi, Fred.
Fred (*Looks at audience knowingly*): Hi, Herman, did you hear what's happening _____ (date)?
Herman: No, what's happening _____ (date)?
Fred: You mean you really don't know? You haven't gotten a letter or been called or seen any of the notices?
Herman: No.
Fred: Why don't you go downstairs and I'll come down in a minute and tell you what's happening. (**Herman** *exits.*)
Fred (*To audience*): Just so there's no misunderstanding, I want to tell you all now myself. On _____ (date) we're _____ (event), and all of you are welcome. See you there! (*Exits.*)

A Winner

by Judy Simmons

Alice: Hey, Billy. Watcha' doin'?
Billy: Aw, nuthin', Alice. I never do nuthin' on _____ (day of event).
Alice: Me neither, Billy. To tell you the truth, I'm just plain bored.
Billy: Well, have a seat, Alice. It's better to be bored to-gether than to be bored alone.
Alice: Yeah, I guess so. (*Pauses, acting very bored.*)
Alice: You know somethin', Billy?
Billy: What, Alice?
Alice: It's no good to be bored together, either. Let's think of something else we can do.

Billy: Well, we could go skating.

Alice: That's a great idea! (*Jumps up, excited.*) I'll go home and ask Mom and . . . Oh! (*Looks crestfallen.*)

Billy: What's the matter, Alice?

Alice: I can't go skating, Billy. I don't have any skates.

Billy: Oh, Alice. Don't be stupid. You can rent skates at the skating rink.

Alice: Oh, yeah. Neat! Thanks, Billy. You're real smart. (*Starts to exit, then looks sad.*)

Billy: What's the matter, Alice?

Alice: Oh, Billy. I can't go skating. I don't have any money. I used all of my allowance on the movies last week.

Billy: Too bad for you, Alice. I guess you'll just have to be bored. *I'm* going skating. Good-bye, Alice. (*Starts to exit, then looks sad.*)

Alice: What's the matter, Billy?

Billy: Oh, Alice. I can't go skating because I don't have any money, either. (*Turns his pockets inside out.*)

Alice: Too bad, Billy. Well, what else can we do? I'm tired of being bored—it's too boring!

Billy: Well, we could ride our bikes.

Alice: Hey, Billy. That's great! You're sharp. I could just hug you for that!

Billy: Watch it, Alice! I'd rather be bored than hugged by you!

(**Alice** *jumps around, all excited, then looks sad.*)

Billy: What's the matter, Alice?

Alice: You won't believe this. (*Almost crying.*) My bicycle is in the shop getting fixed. I can't go bike riding either.

Billy: Alice, you're a real fun killer. First you hug me; then you say that your bike is broken. Well, just for that, you'll have to think of something fun for us to do.

Alice (*sobs for a while, then jumps up*): I've got it, Billy! The neatest idea in the world! Get up, Billy, and be happy!

Billy: Why? If I'm bored, I can't be happy. It's against the rules of boredom.

Alice: But Billy, I have a marvelous idea!

Billy: You already said that, Alice. Tell your idea, don't just talk about it!

Alice: Let's talk together! That way, we won't have to be bored anymore.

Billy: Talk! (*Shocked.*) Talk! Stupid girl thinks talking is fun—good grief!

Alice (*Cries*): Oh, Billy!

(*Another puppet enters, whistling. His name is the same as the project being promoted. He is "cool"—the perfect young man.*)

Project: Hello, everyone. What seems to be your trouble? (**Alice** *keeps crying.*)

Billy: We're bored. (*Puts head down.*)

Project: Well, I guess I'll have to go into action. (*Straightens up, whistles. Several puppets enter.*)

Girl: Hello. Do you need us?

Project: Yes, kids. We've got a bad case of (project day) blues. Do you know what to do?

Boy: Of course. Ready, everyone? NOW! (*New puppets join hands and shout as a cheering squad—boys and girls might separate on parts and then join in together on the end.*)

All: We've got something to share.
We've got something that's rare.
A chance for fellowship
A chance for fun
A chance to grow for everyone
Come if you dare!
Where? Where?
(Name of Project) (Repeat Project Name)
(**Billy** *and* **Alice** *slowly look up. They are puzzled at first, but other puppets begin chattering all at once about activities in the project.*)

Billy (*Shouts*): Wait a minute! Wait a minute! (*Everything gets suddenly quiet.*)

Billy: How much does all this great stuff cost?

Project: It's free, man, free!

Billy: Well, where is it? Do we have to go far?

Project: It's right in your neighborhood. It's being held at ___ (*your church's name or place*).

Alice: How long does it last?

Project: About (*Length of project*).

Alice: Let's go, Billy. It's worth a try.

Billy: Yeah. I'll try your (*name of project*). You say it happens (date)? That's great! Now Alice and I won't have to be bored! We can have fellowship with ya'll.

Project: OK everyone, one more time! (*Puppets join hands with* **Billy** *and* **Alice**.)

All: We've got something to share.
We've got something that's rare.
A chance for fellowship
A chance for fun
A chance to grow for everyone
Come if you dare!
Where? Where?
(Name of project) (Repeat name of project)

The Best Storybook

by Marianne Hawkins

(**Freddie, Ralph,** *and* **Susie** *enter and watch* **Johnnie** *as he reads.* **Johnnie** *says, "Wow! Fantastic! How exciting!" and so forth.*)

All: What are you readin', John?
What's so interesting?
Is it a monster story?
Is it about cowboys?
Lemme see!
Tell us about it!
Yeah, tell us.
Hey, let me see!

Johnnie (*Excitedly*): I am reading some of the best stories that were ever written! They are true stories. Things that really happened a long time ago!

Freddie (*Eagerly*): I knew they were cowboy stories!

Ralph: Tell us about 'em, John!

Susie: Give me the book . . . I want to see. (**Susie** *looks at book; the other puppets gather around her.*)

Freddie: Wait a minute, Johnnie. That's not a storybook.

Ralph: Yeah . . . that's a *Bible!*

Johnnie: I know! And all the stories in it really happened. Just like I said!

Susie (*Giggles*): Hey, you're right! The Bible is God's Word, and it is absolutely true!

(*All nod agreement.*)

Freddie: What were you reading about, John?

Johnnie: About the time that Jesus healed the blind man. He had never been able to see anything in his whole life, and Jesus made him well!

Susie (*Looks at Bible*): Here are the verses that tell about Jesus calming the storm on the sea when the disciples thought they were gonna drown!

Ralph: Hey . . . remember the story about how Jesus fed over five thousand people with just one little boy's lunch?

Freddie: How about the time he made the demons come out of the man that was crazy?

Johnnie: There are lots and lots of stories about Jesus' miracles. He was God's Son, and he had all power and knowledge.

Ralph (*Quietly*): But you know what? Jesus never did those miracles to be a show-off. He did them to help people.

Susie: That's right, Ralph. Jesus didn't want attention. He just wanted to show people how much he loved them.

Johnnie: I think the greatest miracle of all is that Jesus loves all of us so much that he was willing to die for us on the cross! Just think, he did that years and years before we were even born!

Freddie: You're right, Johnnie. God's love for sinners is the greatest miracle of all.

Ralph: But don't forget! The story doesn't end there! Jesus died, but he rose from the grave! That's another miracle!

Susie: That's right! The Bible tells about all the people who saw Jesus and talked to him after his resurrection!

Freddie: Jesus is alive in heaven right now!

Ralph: And he lives in the hearts of all Christians—like you and me!

Johnnie: Why don't we take my Bible and go tell our friends about Jesus and his miracles?

Others: Yeah! That's a good idea! Jesus loves them, too! Come on, let's go!

(*All exit.*)

God's Road Map

by W. H. Voorhes and Joey

V: Hi, everyone. How are you this morning? And good morning to you, Joey. How are you today?

J: I'm fine. How are you?

V: Fine, thank you.

J: You're welcome.

V: Say, Joey, I thought we'd do something a little different today. I thought that we could hold an interview.

J: What's an interview?

V: That's where someone asks questions and the other person answers them.

J (*To audience*): I bet I can guess who's got to answer the questions.

V: Oh, come on, Joey, they'll be easy questions. For instance, "Where did you come from?"

J: That's easy. I came from California.

V: California? It's clear across the country—a long way away. Joey, how did you get here from California?

J: I came in a truck.

V: I wonder how the truck driver found his way here? I couldn't find my way to California.

J: You could if you had what the truck driver had.

V: What did he have?

J: He had a road map.

V: Oh, yes, I've used road maps before. I'm sure everyone has seen road maps before, haven't you? They guide us to the place we want to go and tell us how to go there the best way. Joey, did you realize that God has a road map?

J (*To audience*): I knew the questions would get harder. (*Shakes head.*) No, I didn't know that God had a road map.

V: He does. He has a road map for everyone. It's not quite like the truck driver's road map, but it does tell us the way we should go in order to be the person that God wants us to be.

J: Oh, now I know what you're talking about! You're talking about God's Holy Word, the Bible!

V: That's right, Joey, God's Bible is his road map for our lives. The Bible tells us how God wants us to live and act and grow. (*To audience.*) If you want to know how God wants you to live and act and grow, and how to please him, then you need to read your Bible every day.

J: I know a song about the Bible; can I sing it with the audience?

V: Sure, everyone join in along with Joey:

J: Oh, "The B-I-B-L-E, that's the book for me, I'll stand alone on the Word of God, The B-I-B-L-E."

V: Very good; but now, Joey, I think we'd better say good-bye.

J: OK. So long, everyone. Talk to you next week.

The Library

by Mary Lou Serratt

1: Man, what a dull day . . . wish I had something really super to do. Hey! (*Looks offstage.*) Here comes Joey. Maybe he can think of something different to do. (*Calls offstage.*) Hey, Joey . . . man, I'm glad to see you. Hurry on over here 'cause I need your help.

2 (*Begins speaking offstage*): I'm comin', just give me a minute. This is Saturday, haven't you heard? You're not supposed to hurry on Saturday! (*Enters, carrying Bible.*) In fact, I'm plannin' a nice, lazy morning.

1: You are? (*Aside to audience.*) Well, that sounds a little strange, but then I wanted to do something different. (*To Joey.*) You don't mean you're gonna sleep all day, do you?

2: Naw. See that tree over there? Well, I'm goin' to take this sack of cookies and my library over there and just enjoy myself.

1: Huh? I see the cookies; but what do you mean, your library? All I see is that one book. Now, I'm not much on books, but even I know that it takes more than one to have a library. (*To audience.*) I'd move on right now 'cept for one thing . . . I've tasted his mom's cookies before!

2: That book is my library. It's new, too. (*Could ad-lib here about who gave it to him and that the group will give his friend one too, if it is applicable.*) I don't know a lot about it, but I know it's not one book . . . not really. It's 66 books all together in a portable library, sorta.

1 (*To audience*): This I cannot believe. (*To Joey.*) OK, Joey, just prove to me there are 66 books in your hand. If you can do that I won't even ask for a cookie!

2: Well, right in front are the names . . . 39 in a group called the Old Testament; 27 in a group called the New Testament. There are some really neat stories in here. It's special, you see, 'cause God told men to write it.

1: That sounds like dullsville to me. I don't think even those cookies would make it worth some old-timey stuff like that.

2 (*Continues*): Last night I read this story about a guy named Daniel. He was real young, see, but he believed in God and did everything God told him to do, even when he was a sorta prisoner. Well, he got thrown in a pit with some lions and everybody thought sure he'd end up a pile of bones, but that ole lion didn't even scratch Daniel 'cause God was taking care of him.

1: Hey, you didn't tell me it was a book of fairy tales! (*To audience.*) That sounds pretty neat.

2: Oh, it's not. Everything in this library is true. Even the story of this guy named Noah. He built a big ship, bigger than a football field, and loaded it up with all kinds of animals—rats and dogs and birds and elephants and tigers and . . .

1: (*Interrupting*): And skunks, I suppose . . . (*Laughing.*)

2: That's right. In fact, if it hadn't been for Noah and what God helped him do, we wouldn't have any animals now. In fact, we wouldn't be here! Right now I'm gonna go read a story about this kid named David. He's going to fight a giant. Doesn't seem like he'd have a chance, but Jack read it; and he says David killed that giant and ended up being a king!

1: Wow, man. That sounds like a pretty neat book, uh, oops, I mean library. Think I could come along and find out how that kid could do that? He must be the hero, huh?

2: Well, I guess you could say he's one of the heroes. God can help even kids do things that seem impossible to everybody. He could even make us heroes if we learned to obey him. I'm trying to learn about what God could help me do. That's one reason I want to spend some time reading his library. It'd be more fun to read together, and I have plenty of cookies . . . . (*Starts offstage, followed by* **no. 1.**)

ENDING 1

1 (*As they exit.*): Now, how did you say that guy got all those animals on one boat? I mean, where did he put those skunks!?

ENDING 2

1: Great, I want to hear about that library . . .

2: Well, one good place to learn more about it is at Sunday School every Sunday morning at 9:45 AM (*or other time*). (*To audience.*) Hey, why don't you plan to come, too?

Johnnie's Suitcase

by Marianne Hawkins

(**Johnnie** *and* **Susie** *enter together.*)

Johnnie: Boy, I can't wait for our trip to Grandma's. School is almost out for the weekend. I'm so excited!

Susie: Me too, Johnnie! I can hardly wait. Are you all packed and ready to go?

Johnnie: No, I can't find my suitcase. Have you seen it? (*Looks around.*) I guess I had better go look for it. (*Exits.*) Maybe it's in the closet.

Susie (*To audience*): That's Johnnie for you. Always putting things off until the last minute.

Johnnie (*Offstage*): Susie, hey Susie! I found it!

Susie (*To audience*): Finally!

Johnnie (*Enters, whistling*): Well, I got all my clothes packed!

Susie: Just in time too!

Johnnie: And I packed my toothbrush!

Susie (*Hesitantly*): Uh . . . that's great, Johnnie, but uh . . . we don't have any teeth! (*Both puppets turn slowly toward audience.*)

Johnnie: Well, I believe in being prepared! I also packed my hairbrush and comb.

Susie: It looks like you need to use it!

(**Johnnie** *acts shocked.*)

Susie: Wow, Johnnie! With all that stuff in your suitcase, I'll bet it is pretty full. You'll probably have to sit on it to get it closed.

Johnnie: I guess I will. Well, I've got to go finish packing. All I need now is to pack my sword and my shield, my lamp, my book of hymns, my bread, my guide, my library of 66 books, a group of letters, and . . .

Susie (*Interrupts*): What? Are you kidding? You can't mean it!! There's no way you could . . . Wait a minute. (*Flops over edge of stage.*) There's no way that you can do that! Do you expect me to believe that you are going to put 66 books, a lamp, a bunch of letters, and all that other stuff in one little suitcase? It would take a dump truck to hold all of that! You can't do it!!

Johnnie: Oh, yes I can!

Susie: I don't believe it. How in the world can you possibly get all of . . .

Johnnie (*Interrupts*): Just wait right here, Susie. I'll show you. (*Exits.*)

Susie (*To audience*): He can't possibly do that. There is no way! Sixty-six books, a lamp . . . how dumb does that guy think I am!

Johnnie (*Returns, carrying a Bible*): See, Susie, everything I named is right here . . . in my Bible!

(**Susie** *looks unbelieving, turns to audience.*)

Johnnie: It has 66 books, and Psalms is a book of hymns. The Bible is a lamp because it says in Psalms 119:105 that God's Word is a "lamp to my feet and a light to my path." That means that it helps me to know what God wants me to do.

Susie: Yeah . . . and the Bible is called the Sword of the Spirit too.

Johnnie: It's a very important book, Susie. I love my Bible because it has so many wonderful stories in it and because it is God's Word.

Susie: I need to go pack *my* Bible in my suitcase, Johnnie!

Johnnie: Let's go tell Mom what we have packed!

Susie (*Giggles*): Yeah . . . 66 books, a lamp . . .

Johnnie: She'll never believe us!

(*Both exit, laughing.*)

Do You Go to Church?

by Walter Norvell

(Perform this skit as though a TV newscaster is on the street interviewing passersby.)

Charlie Chuckles: Hello out there to our TV audience. This is Charlie Chuckles of W_ _ _ (insert the initials of your church for the call letters of the station) bringing you "The Voice of the Man in the Street." Today we are interviewing people at the corner of _____ and _____. (Insert a local intersection.) Our question for today is, "Do you go to church?" Here comes our first person. Good day, Ma'am. I'm Charlie Chuckles of W_ _ _. May I have your name?

Mrs. Toobusy: I'm Priscilla Toobusy. Please hurry, young man; I'm quite busy!

Charlie Chuckles: OK. Our question for today is, "Do you go to church?"

Mrs. Toobusy: Well, quite honestly, young man, I go to church when I'm not too busy. I'm involved in so many fine social organizations. I work with the Children's Home, the Volunteer Helpers, the Civic League, the Help Conserve Our Southern Grubworm Association—by the way, we're having a raffle to raise money to send some poor little grubworms to Hawaii for educational purposes. I just happen to have 600 raffle tickets with me. Would you . . .

Charlie Chuckles: Mrs. Toobusy, how often do you attend church?

Mrs. Toobusy: Oh, I attend regularly, every Christmas and Easter. Well, I didn't attend last Easter because I was so busy, the holiday just slipped up on me. I didn't even get a new dress. I despise attending without fine new clothes. Why, I might look (Gasp) commonplace! (Hurries off.)

Charlie Chuckles: Well, thank you, Mrs. Toobusy. I'm sure you need to hurry along. Here comes another person. Sir—oh, Sir. Do you have a minute? I'm Charlie Chuckles of W_ _ _. Could you answer our question for today?

Man: Sure, just ask.

Charlie Chuckles: Do you go to church?

Man: Well . . . I have a business of my own . . . and I'm a family man. I try to be with my kids when I don't have to work. You know how we small businessmen are—struggling just to keep above water. With taxes and high utilities I have to work seven days a week just to put bread on the table. But I don't have to work every Sunday. For my days off we bought a little camper for the family to enjoy—$20,000. We drive it to the lake where we keep our ski boat. Hardly ever use it more than three weekends a month. Why, just the other day, I told Martha she ought to take the boys to Sunday School when I work.

Charlie Chuckles: Thank you, sir. Here's another. Pardon me . . . Mister?

Hippie: Huh? Yeah, man, what's on your mind, man? Spill it.

Charlie Chuckles: I'm Charlie Chuckles of W_ _ _. Our question for the day is, "Do you go to church?"

Hippie: Church, man? You have got to be kidding. Where have you been? That church stuff is old, even dead, man. Get it together, friend. Worship what you want when you want. That church stuff is for people with no brains—run by people out for money. Its just a plastic front. Now, take me, man. I worship all along, everywhere. I'm a religious person! When I find that high, I discover God all around me. Man, that's beautiful!

Charlie Chuckles: Well, then . . . when did you worship last?

Hippie: Let me see, . . . I was with some friends . . . we were sittin' around transcending and meditating . . . I guess that was about two years ago.

Charlie Chuckles: I see! Hummm . . . thank you very much. Here comes another young man. Let's see if I can get his opinion. Hey, fella . . .

Young Man: Yes, what can I do for you?

Charlie Chuckles: I'm Charlie Chuckles of W_ _ _. Would you mind answering our question of the day?

Young Man: No, not at all. Go ahead.

Charlie Chuckles: The question is, "Do you go to church?"

Young Man: Yes.

Charlie Chuckles (Surprised): How often do you attend?

Young Man: As often as I can. My church has Wednesday night services as well as the services on Sunday morning and night.

Charlie Chuckles (Very surprised): You're the first person I've interviewed who answered like this. Can you explain why you go to church?

Young Man: Well, to begin with, my parents were active, so I just sorta grew up at church. But my main reason is more than that. When I was a teenager I met Jesus Christ and took him as my Savior. I discovered that that one act made me a child of God and a member of his church. It only seemed natural that if I was committed to that man Jesus, I should serve in his church. I've tried to do that ever since—with his help.

Charlie Chuckles: Well, that's an answer I hadn't expected. Could you hang around a minute? I'd like to talk with you some more.

Young Man: Sure.

Charlie Chuckles: Well, that about wraps up our show for today. This is Charlie Chuckles of W_ _ _ asking you today's question—"Do you go to church?"

Witnessing?

by Debbie Smith

(*Four separate scripts, performed consecutively*)

Script 1
(*Two puppets enter; 1 rushes over to 2.*)
1: Excuse me, sir, but I have a question for you. If you died right now, do you know for sure where you would go?
2: Huh?
1: Sir, do you know that if you died right now that you would go to heaven?
2: Well, uh . . .
1: Did you know that you are a sinner and destined for hell if you don't repent? (*Yells.*) SINNER! TURN OR BURN!
(*2 shakes as other puppet is over him.*) (*Exit.*)

Script 2
(*Two puppets enter.*)
2: Praise the Lord! Amen, brother! Thank you, Jesus! (*Sees other puppet.*) Well, praise the Lord, how ya doin' there?
1: To tell ya the truth, not very well lately.
2: Well, praise the Lord anyway.
1: I've been having so many problems. It seems like the whole world is against me.
2: Amen, brother. Just praise the Lord, anyway. Turn the problems over to Jesus, that's all. Praise the Lord, Amen! Praise . . . the . . . Lord!!! (*Exits.*)
1 (*To audience*): Jesus who? (*Exits.*)

Script 3
(*2 enters, walking by 1.*)
1: Hey, hey . . .
2: You talking to me?
1: Yes, I am. I really need someone to talk to.
2: Well, I'd love to stop, but I'm off to my church's softball practice.

1: Listen, I really need to talk these problems out. Is there anytime this week when you could come and talk to me?
2: Well, let me see. Tomorrow is visitation, and Wednesday is prayer meeting; Thursday is discipleship group; Friday we are having a churchwide fellowship; and Saturday the youth are all going to the beach. And everybody knows that Sunday is the Lord's day!
1: Well, I'm sorry to have bothered you.
2: Oh, no bother. Anytime, just let me know.
(*Exits.*)

Script 4
1 (*Enters alone*): Lord, we've been studying at church how you command each Christian to be a witness. Lord, please give me an opportunity to witness today. Thank you. Amen.
2 (*Enters during the prayer*): Who were you talking to?
1: Who? Me?
2: Yes, I know I heard you talking to somebody. Who was it?
1: Uh, uh, well uh, the Lord. (*Softly and quickly.*)
2: The who?
1: The, the, the Lord? (*Like a question.*)
2: The Lord, whose Lord?
1: Just the Lord.
2: What's his name?
1: Jesus.
2: Oh! Yes! I've heard about him. Could you tell me more about him? I really want to know.
1: Well, uh, why don't I go get my pastor or my youth director? Maybe they can come tell you more about Jesus tomorrow or maybe next week. (*Exits.*)
2 (*Pauses*): But I'm not going to be here tomorrow. (*Exits.*)

Fishers of Men

by Marianne Hawkins

Susie (*Enters, calls loudly*): Johnnie, oh Johnnie! That boy is never here when I need him! (*Calls again.*) Johnnie!
Johnnie (*from offstage*): Don't be such a loudmouth, Susie. I'm coming just as fast as I can! (*Comes onstage, speaks haltingly, as if out of breath.*) What . . . (*Pants*) . . . did . . . you . . . want . . . Susie? I . . . was . . . way . . . down

. . . the . . . street. (*Puppets face each other as they talk.*)
Susie: Oh, it wasn't very important. I just wanted you to go to the park with me. We could fly a kite or something. Isn't that a good idea?
Johnnie: Uh . . . yeah, Susie. That sounds like fun. But I've got something important to do. I'm going fishing! I was on

my way when I heard you calling.

Susie: Fishing! Johnnie—you don't even like fish! You won't eat it when your mom cooks it. Why would you want to waste a beautiful day by going fishing?

Johnnie: Oh, Susie, I wouldn't be wasting time. It's one of the best ways I know to spend my time.

Susie: I don't understand you, Johnnie. Besides, if you were going fishing you'd need a fishing pole and lots of other stuff!

Johnnie: Susie, I've got everything I need . . . right here in my pocket. (*Pats shirt with one hand as he speaks.*)

Susie (*Shows surprise*): What do you mean, Johnnie? There's not room in your pocket for a fishing pole and fishing line and . . . oh no, Johnnie . . . you wouldn't . . . you couldn't . . . Johnnie!

Johnnie: What, Susie?

Susie (*Weakly*): You wouldn't put WORMS in your pocket would you? Eich!!! (**Susie** *trembles.*)

Johnnie (*Snickers*): No, Susie . . . I promise you that I don't have worms in my pocket. In fact, I don't have any of the things you named in my pocket . . . no fishing pole, no line . . . nothing like that!

Susie: Then how can you catch any fish? You've got to use something!

Johnnie: You're right. That's why I have my Bible right here in my pocket. I can sure be a fisherman with my Bible.

Susie: What in the world are you talking about? Oh . . . wait a minute there, Johnnie. What kind of fish are you trying to catch?

Johnnie: I thought you'd guess, Susie. Jesus said in Matthew 4:19, "Follow me, and I will make you fishers of men." That means because I'm a Christian I want to tell other people about Jesus.

Susie: That's the *best* kind of fishing, Johnnie! And your Bible is the right way to catch "people fish." It tells all about how Jesus loves us and how to ask him to come into our hearts and save us!

Johnnie: You're right, Susie! Hey—would you like to go fishing with me? Fishing for men!

Susie: Sure! What are we waiting for? Let's go!
(*They exit.*)

Be Prepared

by Marianne Hawkins

Johnnie (*Enters alone, talks to himself*): Hmmm . . . let me see . . . what was that memory verse again? Oh, yeah! "Prepare ye the way of the Lord, make his paths straight." Wow! John the Baptist sure was a brave man. I wish I could be like him. (*Recites loudly—as if pretending he was John the Baptist.*) "Prepare ye the way of the Lord."

Susie (*Enters while* **Johnnie** *is talking*): Hey, Johnnie, wasn't that our new memory verse I heard you saying?

Johnnie: Yeah, Susie! "Prepare ye the way of the Lord, make his paths straight" (Luke 3:4).

Susie: That's good, Johnnie. I'm glad you learned that verse. You know, John the Baptist was a very important man because he really did prepare the way for Jesus. He went all around the countryside telling everyone about Jesus!

Johnnie: I know! He worked very hard to make sure that everyone knew that Jesus was coming.

Susie: Well, you know what I've been thinking about?

Johnnie: No, what?

Susie: Is there anything we can do in today's world to "prepare the way of the Lord"?

Johnnie: Sure there is, Susie. We can do the same thing John the Baptist did!

Susie: You mean telling everyone about Jesus and how much he loves them?

Johnnie: Yes, Susie! Because Jesus is going to come back someday, and he wants everyone to be saved.

Susie: That's right, Johnnie. It says that in the Bible.

Johnnie: We can witness just like John the Baptist did.

Susie: Yeah . . . Hey, wait a minute! (*Snickers.*) JOHN—So that's what you were doing when I came in!

Johnnie (*Sheepishly*): What do you mean?

Susie: You were pretending to be John the Baptist. (*Laughs again.*)

Johnnie: Well . . . after all . . . my name is John.

Susie: Oh, brother! (*Snickers.*)

Johnnie (*Shocked*): What are you laughing at? John the Baptist was a very brave man. He was so strong and big! It would be great to be like him!

Susie: Aw . . . I'm just teasing, Johnnie. (*Moves closer to him and speaks admiringly.*) Besides, you'll grow up to be big and strong some day.

Johnnie: What do you mean, someday? Just look at this muscle! (*Flexes arm.*)

Susie: Oh, Johnnie, I give up! (*Exits.*)

Johnnie (*Exits saying*): "Prepare ye the way of the Lord."

Stewardship

by Sam Sanders

Preacher: It is my pleasure to talk to you wonderful folks this evening on the subject "Good things about our church." And we do have many, many good things in our church.
Group (*All speak at once*): AAAAmen! Uuuuuuuh huh! Right on! Preach on! Amen!
Preacher: One good thing about our church is the preaching ministry . . . heh, heh, heh.
  (**Group** *gives same response as above.*)
Preacher: We preach the Word! We believe the Bible is true!
  (**Group** *gives same response as above.*)
Preacher: Another good thing about this church is that we emphasize evangelism!
  (**Group** *gives same response as above.*)
Preacher: We think evangelism is important because the Bible teaches us that we should tell the story of Jesus to everyone, and seek to make all men disciples . . . .
  (**Group** *gives same response as above.*)
Preacher: And we consider music to be very, very important to our church . . . .
  (**Group** *gives same response as above.*)
Preacher: Music is worship, Scripture, praise, thanks, and a proven crowd-gatherer!
  (**Group** *gives same response as above.*)
Preacher: And we consider our stewardship emphasis to be one of the most important programs in our church!
  (**Group** *gives a motionless, stony silence.*)
Preacher (*Surprised, pauses*): Wh, wh . . . what happened to all the amens?
  (**Group** *look at each other, mumble.*)
1: Uh . . . did, ah . . . you say, uh . . . ahem . . . stewardship . . . ?
Preacher: Why, yes . . . yes, of course I did.
2: Well, preacher, we don't like to talk about, uh . . . stewardship . . .

Preacher: You don't? Why not?
3: Why not? Because, preacher, when you say stewardship . . . you really are talking about the Big "M," aren't you?
Preacher: The Big "M"?
4: Yes . . . you know, the Big "M" . . . MONEY! And that makes it very, very personal . . .
1: Right! A Christian's money is a matter between him and God . . .
2: Yes, it's nobody else's business.
Preacher: What? You people sound like the type who wouldn't sign a pledge card. Right?
4: That's right, Preacher. But remember, it doesn't say anything in the Bible about pledge cards! (*Group mutters agreement.*)
Preacher: Maybe it doesn't say anything specifically about pledge cards . . . but it doesn't say anything about printed literature either. And we use that, don't we? The Bible doesn't mention projectors and microphones and typewriters and many other things, but we use them because it helps us do the Lord's work better through his church. Our stewardship program simply helps us do the Lord's work more effectively by making the best use of his tithes and our offerings.
Group (*Impressed, mumble to each other*): Hmmmmmm . . . Welllllll . . . Never thought about that . . . maybe . . .
Preacher: It's still a personal matter, between an individual and God; but doing the work of the Lord is personal, too. And I can't help but believe that God would have us do everything we can to help our church to minister to this community. Now . . . where was I? Ah, yes . . . (*Preaching again.*) We consider stewardship one of the most important programs in our church!
Group (*Pause momentarily, look at each other, then blurt out*): Amennnnn! Right on! Preach on, brother! Yessir! (*They exit.*)

Diggin' Deeper

by Greg George

1 (*Looking in a box with word DEEP on it*): Deeper, deeper, a little deeper.
2: What are you doing?
1: I'm doing what the preacher said to do. (*Goes back in box.*)
2: You're doing what the preacher said?

1: Yeah, I'm digging deeper.
2 (*Surprised*): What do you mean, you're digging deeper?
1: The preacher says we need to dig a little deeper this year if we're going to meet our budget. (*Goes back into box.*) So I'm digging deeper.
2: That's not what the preacher meant.

1 (*Shocked, head pops out of box*): It's not?

2: No, the preacher meant we all need to be tithers.

1: Oh! Well, hold on just a minute. (*Exits and comes back with a tie and throws over front rail.*) There we are.

2: What's that?

1: That's a tie.

2: A tie—what did you bring that up for?

1: To show the preacher that I'm a tie-er, like you said.

2: Are you crazy?

1: I don't know; how do you tell?

2: I didn't say a tier; I said a tither.

1: A tither? What's a tither?

2: You see, that's part of the problem. People don't know what a true tither is.

1: You must be kidding. I know what a tither is; it's a person who gives money to the church.

2: No, that's not what a tither is.

1 (*A little surprised*): Oh! That's right, a tither is a person who gives money to the church every week.

2: No, I'm afraid you're wrong again.

1 (*Loudly*): Wrong! What do you mean, wrong?

2: Please, don't get all excited. You're not 100 percent wrong. As a matter of fact, you're pretty close.

1 (*Surprised*): I am?

2: Sure, you just need to add a few details. But most people think about like you do.

1: They do?

2: Yeah. Why, there are people who come to church every Sunday dressed in $150.00 suits who tip the Lord a dollar and think they're tithers because they do it every week; but they're not.

1: Well, what are they?

2: Most of them are fine people who love the Lord and his church, but they just have not found the true meaning of being a tither.

1: Tell me then, what is a tither?

2: I thought you would never ask. A tither is an individual who knows the Lord as his Savior and willingly gives at least 10 percent of his income to the Lord, not to mention his time and talents.

1: I see! So when the preacher says we need to dig deeper, he means we all need to be tithers and give at least a tenth to the Lord.

2: That's exactly right; you can't have a church this size without people who are faithful with their money.

1: Man, I really understand how important tithing is now.

2: You do?

1: Sure. Why, if it weren't for people tithing and giving to their church, then the church couldn't have a puppet ministry; and without that we wouldn't be here. (*To audience.*) Please, if you're not a tither, start tithing for our sake and yours.

Stewardship

by Marianne Hawkins

(**Susie** *and* **Freddie** *enter and ad-lib as* **Johnnie** *rushes up to them.*)

Johnnie (*Frantically*): Susie, you won't believe the terrible thing that's happened to me!

Susie (*Concerned*): What's wrong, Johnnie?

Freddie: Yeah, what happened?

Johnnie: The pastor asked me to give my testimony in church Sunday night! Isn't that awful?

Freddie: In front of all those people? Wow . . that *is* awful!

Susie (*Glares at Freddie*): Hush, Freddie—you're not helping things at all!

Freddie (*Meekly*): Sorry about that!

Susie: Now calm down, Johnnie. You can do it!

Johnnie (*Moans*): But Susie, he wants me to talk about stewardship!

Freddie: What's *that?*

Susie (*Disgustedly*): Freddie, please!

Freddie (*Meekly*): Sorry about that!

Johnnie (*Ignoring Freddie*): That's the whole problem, Susie. How can anyone explain what stewardship really means?

Susie: You could always start by telling people that they should give their money to the church. You know—giving God back some of what he has given us.

Freddie: I have an idea!

(**Johnnie** *and* **Susie** *ignore him.*)

Johnnie: But isn't stewardship *more* than giving money?

Freddie (*Persistently*): Hey, I have an idea!

Susie (*Still ignoring Freddie*): Of course it is, Johnnie! People should also give of themselves.

Freddie (*Loudly*): Hey, I really have a good idea!

(**Susie** *and* **Johnnie** *both turn to him.* **Johnnie** *sighs and then gives in.*)

Johnnie: OK, let's hear your big idea.

Freddie (*Eagerly*): Why don't you dress up like an empty offering envelope and tell the people how neglected you are?

Susie: Oh, brother. (*Turns away.*)

Johnnie (*Kindly*): Uh . . . thanks anyway, Fred, but I really don't think that's what the pastor had in mind!

Freddie (*Sulking*): Well, I still think it's a good idea!

Susie (*Chuckles*): You would! Anyway, Johnnie, stewardship *is* much more than giving money.

Johnnie: Shouldn't people be willing to give of their *time?*

Susie: And their talents!

Johnnie: God deserves the best of everything we have to offer. I guess that is what stewardship really means.

Freddie (*Insists*): I still think you should dress up like an empty envelope.

Susie (*Interrupts Freddie*): Freddie, if you say that one more time, I am going to put *you* in an envelope and seal it up!

Freddie (*Laughs*): Hey, Susie, that's the best idea you've had all day. Just look at all the talent and brains the church would be getting!

Susie (*Covers head with hands*): I give up . . .

(**Freddie** *and* **Johnnie** *both laugh.*)

Freddie: I was just teasing, Susie!

Johnnie: Well anyway, thanks for helping me think about what to say Sunday night. I'm not so scared now.

Freddie: No trouble, pal. Glad to be of service! (*Exits.*)

Susie (*Laughing*): I'm going to go find *his* empty envelope and mail him to the Foreign Mission Field!

Johnnie (*Chuckles*): Now Susie, that wouldn't be fair to all those hard-working missionaries! Come on, let's go over to my house. I want to look up some Bible verses to use in my testimony.

Susie: OK, Johnnie. That's a good idea.

(*Both puppets exit.*)

Something Special

by Greg George

Bart: Boy oh boy, this must be my lucky day. I walk out of church and spot a bright one-dollar bill, and it's all mine.

Jeff: Did you say you found a dollar?

Bart: That's right, and here it is. (*Holds bill in front of Jeff's face.*)

Jeff: Say, why don't you buy *us* a couple of hamburgers and a cola to celebrate? After all, I am your best friend.

Bart: Gosh, Jeff, if I did that I wouldn't have anything to celebrate.

Jeff: What's money for if you're not going to spend it?

Bart: I didn't say I wouldn't spend it.

Jeff: Oh! Well, come on. I can taste those hamburgers now.

Bart: *However*, I do think I need to consider the various ways I could spend this dollar.

Jeff: Various ways, huh? (*Both silent as if thinking.*) I've got it!

Bart: What have you got?

Jeff: Another way for you to spend your dollar. Instead of buying hamburgers, why not buy *us* a couple of hot fudge sundaes with extra nuts?

Bart: Can't you think of anything but food? Here I have the good fortune of finding a one-dollar bill, something I didn't expect or plan on, and all you want to do is spend it on food.

Jeff: Yeah, I guess you're right. Food is probably a dumb idea. Two minutes after the money is spent the food will be gone anyway. (*Sighs, dreamily looks into distance.*)

Bart: I want to do something really special with this dollar.

Jeff (*Still dreamily looking into distance*): Well, we could have gotten a chili-ham-dog special—now that's special!

Bart: A chili-ham-dog special? What's that?

Jeff: That's a hamburger with chopped hot dog in it, smothered in chili, and topped with a sesame seed bun.

Bart: Oh, *yuck!* (**Candy** *enters.*)

Candy: OK, so I'm not a raving beauty, but I've never gotten that kind of reaction before.

Bart: I'm sorry, Candy, that *yuck* was meant for a chili-ham-dog special.

Candy: That's my favorite.

Jeff: Hey, that's my favorite too. Can you imagine that, two people whose favorite is a chili-ham-dog special?

Candy (*To Bart*): What are you doing waving that dollar bill around?

Bart: Well, it's a kinda long story.

Candy: Then forget it; I haven't got time for a soap opera.

Jeff: Bart here found the money, and *I'm* going to help him spend it.

Candy: In that case count me in. I love spending money.

Bart: But you see, I want to do something *special* with this dollar since I didn't earn it or anything.

Candy: I see!

Bart: You do?

Candy: Sure, you can take me to the amusement park and we'll ride the roller-coaster twice together. That would be real special.

Jeff: Now wait a minute. Where does that leave me?

Candy: Right here! (**Candy** *and* **Jeff** *begin arguing and fussing very loud when* **Pastor Bishop** *enters.*)

Pastor Bishop: I would appreciate it very much if you kids would stop shouting in front of the church.

Bart: Oh, it's Pastor Bishop.

Pastor: What's this all about, Bart?

Bart: Well, I found this dollar here in front of the church when I came out this morning, and Jeff and Candy want to help me spend it.

Pastor: I see. But apparently there is a difference of opinion on how to spend the money, right?

Bart: Right.

Pastor: May I offer an alternative?

Bart: Sure.

Pastor: Well, as you know, right now we're having our special (*cause*) drive, and every extra penny would be a big help.

Bart: Did you say a very special (*cause*) drive?

Pastor: That's right.

Bart (*Giving* **Pastor Bishop** *the dollar*): Then consider this dollar as my contribution.

Pastor: That's mighty fine, Bart, and I'll take it into the church right now. (*Exits.*)

Jeff: Bart, what about *our* food?

Candy: And *our* ride on the roller-coaster?

Bart: Remember, I said I wanted to use the money for something *special*. Well, what could be more special than the (*cause*) drive?

Jeff: Gee, I guess you're right.

Candy: Yeah, you're right—Hey, I've got a quarter.

Jeff: And I've got a dime.

Candy: Let's go contribute this to the (*cause*) drive. (*Both exit.*)

Bart (*To audience*): How about you; do you have an extra dollar or two? We could use it for our (*cause*) drive. I've got to go now, but I'll see you in church. (*Exits.*)

I Like Me

by J. B. Collingsworth

Rosie (*Into mirror*): I like me. I'm going to keep telling myself that. Maybe that stuff Paul was telling me is true. Maybe God don't make no jerks.

Ben (*Enters, overhears her*): It's true, Rosie. God don't make no jerks. Whoever told you that was right! We're made in his image. Psalm 139:14 says: "We are fearfully and wonderfully made" (NASB).

Rosie: Aw, Ben, that's not true! We're just puppets, and we were made by man.

Ben: You know what I mean. When I say "we" I'm talking about everybody—you know, real people with legs and all.

Rosie: Legs! Why did you have to mention legs?

Ben: What's so wrong with legs? Lots of people have them.

Rosie: But I don't. I want to be like everyone else.

Ben: Then you wouldn't be Rosie. I like you, Rosie.

Rosie (*Whispers*): Well, I love you too, but I still wish I had things other people had.

Ben: You may think that, but I really don't believe that *you* believe that deep down.

Rosie: Yes, I do. I want to be special. I want to be . . . well, I want to be me!

Ben: There! You said it. You want to be you. That's great. That's what God wants. He can use you even as a puppet to tell people about Jesus and his love. You have to let him use you, though. Will you do that?

Rosie: I guess—yes, I know you're right. I will try to be me—even if I don't have legs. I want to pray—will you join me? (*They bow heads.*) Thank you, God, for letting your creations make a puppet like me. Use me, Lord, to tell others about you. Amen.

Section II

BIBLE STUDY

What a Day

by Greg George

1 (*Groaning and sighing*): What a day; what a lousy day.
2 (*Enters*): Boy, what's the matter with you? I mean, you look bad. I know you've never looked great, but you look awful today.
1: The question is not, "What is the matter with me?" The question is, "What is right with this lousy day?"
2 (*Repeats question*): What is right with this lousy day?
1: Yeah, that's what I'd like to know too.
2: Now wait a minute. What is so bad about this day?
1: First, I had a test this morning, I mean an easy test; and I failed it.
2: Well, I'm sorry to hear that, but we all have our bad test days when we don't do so well.
1: Yeah, I know, but then there's Linda.
2: Linda! Are you talking about good-looking Linda who you've got a date with Friday night?
1: No! I'm talking about good-looking Linda who I used to have a date with Friday night. She said she wouldn't go out with a dummy.
2: You're not a dummy.
1: Linda said anyone who failed that easy test we had today is a dummy.
2: Oh, I see. Gosh, I'm sorry to hear about Linda too. But remember the saying, "There's more than one fish in the sea."
1: So do I look like a fish?
2: You know what I mean.
1: Yeah, I know, but then there's my headache.

2: You didn't tell me you had a headache too.
1: That's because I didn't get a headache until you asked me about this lousy day. (*Puts hand on head.*) Oh . . . what a lousy day.
2: Now just hold on there. I'm getting tired of you calling this a lousy day. This isn't a lousy day.
1 (*Dejected*): That all depends on how you look at it.
2: That's exactly my point. The Bible says, "This is the day which the Lord has made, let us rejoice and be glad in it" (Ps. 118:24).
1: The Bible says that?
2: It sure does. So if I were you, I believe I would think twice about calling something the Lord made lousy. Remember, he made you too.
1: You know something?
2: What?
1: I think the Lord knew what he was doing when he made this day. So I failed a test and lost a date with Linda—that's no big deal.
2: Now you're talking.
1: After all, I can always ask Karen out. Boy, I feel better.
2: Wait just a minute now! (*Mad.*) You know good and well Karen is my girl.
1: I was just kidding. Remember, "This is the day which the Lord has made, rejoice and be glad in it."
2 (*Both puppets laugh*): You. Come on, let's go rejoice and be glad over a cola. (*Exit.*)

Somebody's Watching

by Marianne Hawkins

(*This skit may be performed with two puppets or with one puppet and a narrator.*)
Narrator: Have any of you seen Chuck the Churchmouse? I've got a feeling that he's around here somewhere.
(**Chuck** *pops up, looks around, exits.*)
Narrator: I thought so! Chuck, come back here!
Chuck (*Slowly peeks over edge of stage*): Hi there! I didn't

mean for you to see me! I just can't help coming in here on Sundays. I love to hear everybody singing and praying. They are learning so much about Jesus!
Narrator: I think so too, Chuck!
Chuck: And everybody looks so happy! That makes me feel happy too!
Narrator: Did you know that it also makes God happy?

Chuck: It does?

Narrator: Sure! The Bible says, "This is the day which the Lord has made; let us rejoice and be glad in it" (Ps. 118:24).

Chuck: I guess that's right. God made every day!

Narrator: Yes, he did! We should be especially happy on Sunday because that is the day we come to church to worship God.

Chuck: Does that mean we should be happy even when things go wrong . . . like when the bus breaks down or when we don't get to sit with our friends, and things like that?

Narrator: Yes, Chuck! God wants us to be happy all of the time!

Chuck: Well, today I was riding the bus and I saw two little girls talking ugly and fighting with each other! Some other children were complaining because they couldn't sit where they wanted to.

Narrator: Really? I guess they just don't realize that somebody is always listening to them and watching them.

Chuck: You mean . . . . God?

Narrator: Yes, God knows everything we do! He even knows the things we think about. But that's not all! Some-body might be riding that bus who isn't a Christian!

Chuck (*Interrupts*): Oh . . . if he saw children who are supposed to be Christians acting ugly, then maybe he wouldn't want to be one!

Narrator: That's right, Chuck!! If somebody didn't think the Christians acted any different than he did, he wouldn't think he needed to become a Christian.

Chuck: Wow! I guess everytime we start to do something wrong, we'd better remember that somebody is watching.

Narrator: Yes . . . and remember, God knows what we do. The best way to act is to decide what Jesus would have done if he was in the same situation. You can't go wrong that way.

Chuck: I think I'll go find those little girls and tell them what we've been talking about.

Narrator: That's a good idea, Chuck! See you later!

(**Chuck** *exits.*)

Sonlight

by Marianne Hawkins

(*A monologue by* **Chuck the Churchmouse.**)

Chuck: Good morning! How are you today?

I wanted to tell you what happened to me at school the other day! (*Slyly.*) You didn't know that I go to school, did you? Well, I do sometimes. I sneak around and watch all my friends and listen to what they are studying.

The other day, I was hiding in a desk in Science class. The teacher was talking about the moon. I was really upset when I found out that the moon is not made of green cheese! What a disappointment! I was planning on taking a trip on the next rocket that went up there, if I could sneak on board with the astronauts!

Well, really, I did learn a lot about the moon. Did you know that the moon doesn't even have any light of its own? That's right . . . it just reflects the light of the sun. Without the sun, it would just be a cold, dark place. Sunlight is awfully important to the moon. We would never even see it unless it reflected the sunlight.

I think our lives are kind of like the moon. We are sort of cold, dark, and empty unless we reflect *sonlight*. And I mean (*Spells*) S-O-N-light, the Son-of-God light. Jesus said, "I am the light of the world." The light of Jesus shining in our lives helps us to show other people the love of God.

Matthew 5:16 says, "Let your light so shine before men, that they may see your good works and give glory to your Father who is in heaven."

Because we love Jesus, we should act as he would act—that's the way to be a good mirror or reflector of the most important light there is—Sonlight—the light of Jesus.

I had better go now! I have to sneak into church and watch the service. Listen to all the Bible stories and songs so that you can learn to be a good *moon.* See you again next week! (*Exits.*)

Working Together

by Rick Brown

Judy (*Sitting with chin propped on folded hands*): Therefore go and make disciples in all nations (*Pause*), baptizing them into the name of the Father and of the Son and of the Holy Spirit (*Pause*); and then teach these new disciples to obey all the commands I have given you (*Pause*); and be sure of this—that I am with you always, even to the end of the . . . . (*At a loss for last word.*)

Frank (*Enters*): What in the "world" are you doing?

Judy: That's it! Even to the end of the world!

Frank: Huh?

Judy: Oh! I'm just memorizing some verses for Sunday School.

Frank: Good grief! That's no fun!

Judy: Sure it is! My teacher gives us a prize if we learn all of our memory verses, and we get a star on a chart each time we learn a verse.

Frank (*Sarcastically*): Whoopee!

Judy: But best of all—I get to learn what God wants me to do.

Frank: God tells you what he wants you to do through a book?

Judy: Yes! The Bible is God's Word. That's how he talks to Christians.

Frank: What's a . . . Christian?

Judy: Someone who has given his life to Jesus Christ, God's Son.

Frank: Can I become a Christian?

Judy: Sure! All you have to do is ask, and he'll come into your life.

Frank: Is that all?

Judy: Yep!

Frank: Will God tell me what to do through the Bible?

Judy: Sure will.

Frank: See you later. I've got to go tell Chip about this. (*Exits.*)

Judy (*Turning to audience*): So that's what the verse means! "Therefore go and make disciples in all nations, baptizing them into the name of the Father and of the Son and of the Holy Spirit, and then teach these new disciples to obey all the commands I have given you; and be sure of this—that I am with you always, even to the end of the world."

Face Your Problems

by Marianne Hawkins

(**Freddie** *enters whistling or humming.*)

Freddie: Boy, is it a beautiful day! The sun is shining, birds are singing, there's no school—who could ask for a more perfect day? I think I'll go over to Susie's and play for a while.

(**Freddie** *crosses stage, still whistling, and almost collides with* **Johnnie,** *who is running the other way.*)

Freddie: Hey, Johnnie! Where are you going in such a hurry?

Johnnie (*Panting*): I don't know and I don't care! All I know is that I'm getting out of this creepy place!

Freddie (*Shocked*): What do you mean?

Johnnie (*Looks all around to see if anyone is listening*): I'm leaving, Fred. Running away—for good! I'm never going home again!

Freddie (*Quietly*): Now calm down, John. You don't really mean that!

Johnnie: I sure do! I am sick and tired of the hassle that my parents give me. I can't please them . . . nothing I do is right. And school is a real drag and I am sick and tired—

Freddie (*Interrupting*): Now wait a minute, Johnnie. Listen to me! I don't know what happened at your house or why you feel the way you do, but you are making a big mistake!

Johnnie (*Disgusted*): Aw, what do you know about it?

Freddie: All I know is . . . (*Takes a deep breath.*) You're nothing but a big chicken—a coward!

Johnnie (*Angrily*): Now wait a minute—you'd better take that back!

Freddie (*Pleadingly*): Please listen to what I have to say!

Johnnie (*Reluctantly*): OK, but hurry! I don't have any time to waste! And you'd better explain what you meant by calling me a chicken!

Freddie: I called you a chicken because you are running from your problems instead of facing up to them!

Johnnie: Huh?

Freddie: What I am trying to say is this: It takes a lot more courage to solve a problem than to run from it.

Johnnie (*Sarcastically*): Well, that sounds just great, pal, but you don't know what I have to put up with!

Freddie (*Quietly*): Well . . . you're right about that . . . I don't know all your problems. But I do know who can help you solve them.

Johnnie: Yeah? Who?

Freddie: You're a Christian, John. Jesus can help you!

Johnnie (*Hesitantly*): Well, I know, Fred, but sometimes I forget and then . . . . well, how can Jesus help *me*?

Freddie: Do you know what Philippians 4:13 says?

Johnnie: No, I don't think so.

Freddie: It says, "I can do all things through Christ which strengtheneth me." That proves that Jesus can help us face every kind of problem.

Johnnie: I know you are right, Freddie; but when I have a problem, I guess I forget that Jesus will help me.

Freddie: Johnnie, just pray about your problems. Jesus promised to help and he will!

Johnnie: I guess you're right, Freddie. I'm glad I ran into you. I might have really gotten in trouble if you hadn't made me stop and think about what I was doing.

Freddie (*Embarrassed*): Aw, it was nothin'. After all, what are friends for? (**Johnnie** *starts to exit, and* **Freddie** *calls him back.*) Hey, where are you going, Johnnie?

Johnnie: Home, Freddie! Where I belong!

Freddie: I'm glad, Johnnie! Maybe we can play baseball later!

Johnnie: OK, but first I'm going to have a long talk with my mom. I need to tell her I'm sorry for the way I have been acting lately.

Freddie: That's a good idea, John. Well, let's go home. It's almost lunchtime.

(*Both puppets exit, with arms around each other.*)

Nothing Is Impossible

by Tom deGraaf

Sally (*Enters running, breathless*): Oh! Eeh! Whowheee! (*Grabs chest.*) Heavens to high blood pressure! (*Pants.*) . . . I think it's the big one! (*Grabs heart.*) It's the big one!

Dad (*Enters*): . . . It's the big *what*?

Sally: Oh Dad, I think I'm having a heart attack! Oh . . . It's the big one! (*Reels about stage. Suddenly sneezes.*)

Dad (*To audience*): Kind of an *unusual* heart attack . . .

Sally (*Sneezes again*): Aaaaachoooo!

Dad: Another one? And so soon? Shall I call Dr. Welby? How about Dr. Kiley? Ben Casey?

Sally: Well, maybe it's not really a heart attack, but I am going to have one if Freddie Filcher doesn't stop roughing me up! This makes the fourth time this week he's worked me over!

Dad: Do you mean that Freddie Filcher is still picking on you?

Sally: He sure is! Yesterday when all of us were at the lake he was driving the boat while I was skiing behind it, and all of a sudden he swerved toward the shore line and made me ski right over the dock and *into* a thirty-foot houseboat!

Dad (*Shocked*): Freddie did that to you? Well, Sally, what are we going to do about Freddie?

Sally: I don't know—that little monster. I'm going to have a nervous breakup!

Dad: Breakdown . . .

Sally: Well, something's going to break, and I hope it's Freddie!

Dad: Now, Sally, you know it's not nice to make ill wishes toward other people. That means Freddie too.

Sally: But Dad, Freddie Filcher is impossible! There is no way that he can ever be anything other than a complete faux pas! I mean he's just totally bad! He even bought some stained-glass contacts so he could sleep during church!

Dad: Sally, Freddie may sound like an impossible problem to us; but no thing and no one is impossible to God.

Sally: Do you mean I could get God to bust Freddie?

Dad: Sally! You know better than that. What I mean is that God can help people when we can't.

Sally: I'm not sure anybody can help Freddie. Last week he put a fake visitors card in the offering plate at church, and the preacher ended up visiting a 7-11 store!

Dad: I know. I was out visiting with him at the time.

Sally: You? . . . You got fooled too? A haw haw haw . . . (*Laughs uncontrollably.*)

Dad (*Looks slowly at audience*): Just like her mother. (*Pauses, as* **Sally** *laughs on.*) Sally, are you finished?

Sally: (*Stops immediately*): Yes, Dad. I don't know why that struck me so funny. I mean, what's so funny about two grown men actually visiting a 7-11 store as a Sunday School prospect? (*Laughs again.*)

Dad: OK, dear, that's enough. Now it's time we figure out what to do about Freddie.

Freddie (*Backstage*): Sally . . . Oh Sallleeey! Where are you? Wanna go water-skiing some more? A haw haw haw!

Sally: Oh no, Dad! It's Freddie Filcher and he's looking for me again! (*Grabs heart.*) Oh no! It's the big one this time, I know it!

Dad: Sally, you're only six years old and too young for a heart attack. So stop this foolishness!

Sally: Freddie's after me, Dad! What am I going to do? This time he'll probably drown me! I'm doomed!

Dad: Sally, have you already forgotten what I told you a minute ago?

Sally: Yes . . .

Dad: Well, I'll tell you again. No thing or person is impossible for God to handle.

Sally: Are you sure he knows about Freddie, though?

Dad: Now, Sally! God knows about Freddie, and right now I think he wants you to know about one of his verses in the Bible!

Sally: What verse is that?

Dad: Luke 18:27 says, "The things which are impossible with men are possible with God." That means God can change an impossible situation, such as Freddie Filcher.

Freddie (*Backstage*): Oh Salllleeeey—I got the boat all warmed up and ready for you to ski! A haw haw haw.

Sally (*Scared*): I hope God changes him soon!

Dad: Sally, I'm going to ask you to do something very important.

Sally: What?

Dad: I think Freddie is impossible because no one likes him. He has no real family and doesn't go to church very much. I think if someone were to actually be friendly to him and make some effort to understand his problems, he just might turn out to be a nice person after all!

Sally: And you want me to be the guinea pig . . . Well, OK. I'll try. But don't blame me if I come back wiped out!

Dad: Wait a minute, Sally. Let God try! Let's just pray that God gets through to Freddie!

Sally: You said it! (*They pray silently.*) OK . . . here goes! (*Exits.*)

Dad (*To audience*): Well, I know God will help Sally right now as she's talking to Freddie. I know God will because he's carried out a lot of his promises in my days and has given me a strong faith in his Word. As Sally gets older, her faith will grow too as she experiences the trials of life and sees God make the impossible become possible!

Sally (*Enters in a daze*): It's *impossible!*

Dad: What happened? Did he run you into the houseboat again?

Sally: It's impossible! Freddie was actually nice to me . . . (*Dazed.*) It's impossible!

Dad: I knew it all the time! I knew God could change Freddie the "monster" into Freddie the "nice person!"

Sally: He did it! God actually did it! God changed Freddie enough that at least now he said he would come to Sunday School with me; and besides that, he wants to take you water-skiing, Dad!!

Dad (*Stricken*): Me? . . . Water-skiing? . . . With Fre-Fre-Freddie?

Sally: Don't worry, Dad! It's just like you said. God can do the impossible! A haw haw haw! You scared, Dad? Dad, huh? A haw haw!

Dad (*Grabs chest*): It's the big one . . . Here comes the big one! (*Sneezes.*) Aaaaachoooooey!

Sally: Shall I call Dr. Welby? How 'bout Dr. Seuss?

Dad: Never mind—I gotta get to a prayer meeting—*fast!*

Covet? What's That?

by Marianne Hawkins

(**Ralph** *and* **Freddie** *enter and look to one side of stage as if seeing other children playing offstage.*)

Ralph: Boy . . . there goes Johnnie on his new ten-speed bike!

Freddie: Isn't that a great bike? I'm glad Johnnie got it for his birthday.

Ralph: Well, I'm not! He gets everything he wants. (*Bitterly.*) He won't take care of it. He just doesn't deserve a bike like that. It just isn't fair. If I had a bike that pretty, I'd polish it and shine it and put it in the garage at night and . . .

Freddie: Ralph, I bet Johnnie will do all those things too! Why are you so jealous?

Ralph: Whaddya mean, *jealous?* You know as well as I do that Johnnie gets everything he wants. He's got a whole room full of toys and a race-car track and an electric train and now . . . a new ten-speed bike. It just isn't fair for one little kid to have so much stuff—and here we sit with nothin'.

Freddie (*Patiently*): Well, Johnnie's an only child. Maybe that's why he seems to have more things than you do.

Ralph (*Exasperated*): Only child? He's a spoiled brat. All he has to do is ask and his parents rush right out and buy whatever he wants.
Freddie (*Quietly*): "Thou shalt not covet."
Ralph (*Shocked*): Huh?
Freddie: "Thou shalt not covet!"
Ralph: Run that past me just one more time!
Freddie (*With assurance.*): "Thou shalt not covet."
Ralph (*Slowly and deliberately*): What in the world does that mean?
Freddie: It's one of the Ten Commandments.
Ralph: Oh?
Freddie: God told us in the Bible, in Exodus 20:17, to be exact, that we should not covet.
Ralph: He did?
Freddie: Yep!
Ralph: Well? Are you going to tell me what covet means or not?
Freddie (*Chuckles*): OK, pal, it's like this . . . we shouldn't be jealous of the things that other people have. We should be happy with the blessings God gives us instead of comparing what we have with other people.
Ralph: I understand that! But how did you expect me not to do it if I didn't even know what it meant?
Freddie (*Teasingly*): You oughta try listening at church sometime!
Ralph (*Chuckles*): All right, Freddie. That's enough of that!
Freddie: Well, back to Johnnie. You have a lot of things that he doesn't have.
Ralph (*Puzzled*): Like what? He's got everything—new clothes, toys, a big house . . .
Freddie: Just think—you've got a family to play with and go on picnics with and stuff like that. Johnnie doesn't have any brothers or sisters. Can you imagine how lonesome he must get?
Ralph (*Thoughtfully*): I guess I never thought about things that way, Freddie. I do love my big family—I know I would be lonesome without them—even if I had a whole house full of toys. It wouldn't be fun to play by myself all the time.
Freddie: Well, Ralph, everyone has lots of things to be thankful for, if they'll just stop and think about it, instead of being jealous of somebody else.
Ralph: Yeah . . . we shouldn't uh . . . uh . . . covet!
Freddie: Right!
 (**Ralph** and **Freddie** *begin to leave, with* **Ralph's** *final lines fading out as they exit.*)
Ralph: Hey, come on over to my house. My big brother is gonna help me build a treehouse! It's gonna be the best one in town.

The Big Test

by Marianne Hawkins

Susie (*Enters alone, left of stage, crosses to center*): I sure hope Johnnie studied for the big spelling test we're having at school today. It's really going to be hard. (*Looks to right as* **Johnnie** *enters. He is crying.*)
Susie: Johnnie! What's wrong with you?
Johnnie (*Crying*): That mean old bully, Freddie, knocked me down in the mud and tore up my homework because I wouldn't give him my list of spelling words so he could cheat on the test.
Susie: Johnnie, that's awful! What are you going to do?
Johnnie (*Angrily*): I'm going to find him and sock him right in the nose, and then I'm going to get *his* homework and tear it up and stomp it in the mud.
 (*Move puppet up and down as if he was "stomping."*)
Susie (*Shocked*): Johnnie, you can't do that!
Johnnie: Oh yes I can! First I'm gonna sock him and then . . . .
Susie (*Interrupting*): But Johnnie, that's not the way a Christian should act.
Johnnie: Look, Susie, after what Freddie did to me, he deserves to get exactly what I said I was going to give him—a sock in the nose.
 (**Johnnie** *throws a punch with the arm;* **Susie** *jumps away.*)
Susie: Johnnie, you know that's not right!
Johnnie: You can't expect me to be nice to him after what he did to me! I'm really going to get in trouble when my teacher finds out that I don't have my homework. I'll probably fail my spelling test because he tore up the list of words that I was studying! Boy, am I going to get him back!
Susie: Johnnie, don't you know what the Bible says about this?
Johnnie (*Looks slowly around—appears guilty*): Uh, no, Susie . . . what does it say?
Susie: "Love your enemies. Do good to them that despitefully use you." That means to be nice to people even when they are mean to you. That is hard to do, but we should try to do what Jesus said!
Johnnie: Well, I guess that's right. But what am I going to

do about that spelling test? I'm going to fail!

Susie: Why don't you and I go find Freddie and we will help him study. I have a list of the words. You and I can learn by helping him. And maybe next time, we can all work together so Freddie won't have to act that way.

Johnnie: But Susie, look what he did to me—

Susie: Johnnie . . . .

Johnnie: Well, I guess that would be better than punching him in the nose. That wouldn't help any of us to do good on that test.

Susie: Now you're talking, Johnnie. I'm proud of you for making the right decision. Come one, let's go find Freddie. (*Kisses* **Johnnie** *and exits.*)

Johnnie (*Embarrassed*): I'm glad Susie made me think about what the Bible says. I sure do feel better now. Guess I'd better get going so I can learn those words. See you later! (*Exits same direction as* **Susie**.)

School Blues

by Marianne Hawkins

Johnnie (*Enters, looking like he has lost his last friend. Feels sorry for himself*): Oh, this is awful. I just can't stand it! (*Sags over edge of stage.*)

Susie (*Enters*): Johnnie, what in the world is wrong with you?

Johnnie: Oh, Susie, I just can't stand school. We have to sit in there all day instead of playing outside. I can't go swimming or play baseball or do anything fun.

Susie: Now Johnnie, it isn't really *that* bad!! I like my class.

Johnnie: Susie, my teacher gave us homework in every subject. I'll never be able to finish it.

Susie: Wow! Johnnie, that's terrible, but you can do it.

Johnnie: I've got arithmetic and English and social studies and . . .

Susie: Wow! That is a lot of work!

Johnnie: I just won't do it! I think I'll quit school!

Susie: Johnnie, you can't quit school. You know your mother wouldn't let you. Besides, it's against the law to quit school.

Johnnie (*Brightens*): Hey, I've got an idea . . . I'll tell the teacher that a big monster ate up all of my books!

Susie: She wouldn't believe that.

Johnnie: No, I guess not! Hey . . . How about this one? I'll tell her that my dog chewed up all of my paper and pencils!
    (**Susie** *shakes head slowly.*)

Johnnie: No. I guess that wouldn't work either! What am I gonna do?

Susie: Why don't you start by getting to work instead of griping? All you are doing is wasting time. You could be getting through with all that homework instead of complaining.

Johnnie: Yeah, I guess you're right! Oh, well, I guess I should go get my books; but I still don't like the idea.

Susie: Wait a minute, Johnnie! Do you know what the Bible says about studying?

Johnnie: No, Susie, I didn't know it said anything.

Susie: Well, it does! Second Timothy 2:15 says to "Study to show thyself approved unto God, a workman that needeth not to be ashamed."

Johnnie: Oh, Susie, I didn't know that the Bible told us to study. I always want to do what God says is right.

Susie: He wants us always to do our best, Johnnie, at home, at school, and at church. That verse also means that he wants us to study our Bibles too!

Johnnie: Hey, Susie, let's go get our books and study together! That will make it a lot more fun!

Susie: OK, Johnnie, then we can read our Bibles too! (**Johnnie** *and* **Susie** *exit, saying, "Let's do our math first, then our spelling, then the social studies . . . ."*)

And the Winner Is . . .

by Judy George

1st Boy: Hey, what you got there? (*Looking in the distance.*)

2nd Boy (*Enters, running with trophy*): I won! I won! I won this at the scout track meet today! Why weren't you there?

1st Boy: I had things to do.

2nd Boy: What could be more important than winning a trophy or a ribbon?

1st Boy: Man, you didn't listen to the Sunday School teacher Sunday, did you?

2nd Boy: I wasn't there, remember?

1st Boy: That's right; where were you?

2nd Boy (*Boasting*): I was doing a poor old lady a favor.

1st Boy: That was nice.

2nd Boy: I told her if she'd give me ten dollars I'd rake her yard for her. Wasn't that sweet of me?

1st Boy: Why didn't you do it for free since she was poor?

2nd Boy: What kind of person do you think I am? (*Getting angry.*) I'm not doing anything that doesn't give a prize or an award in exchange! I'm not doing anything for free!

1st Boy: Well, I sure do hate even more that you missed Sunday School last Sunday.

2nd Boy: What was so great at Sunday School last Sunday anyway? It's always the same thing, isn't it?

1st Boy: Not if you really listen and want to learn about how God expects us to live. Do you?

2nd Boy: Sure, but . . .

1st Boy: Well, then, I'll tell you what our teacher said since you missed it. But listen closely! In Matthew 6:19-21 Jesus says: "Do not lay up for yourselves treasures on earth, where moth and rust consume and where thieves break in and steal, but lay up for yourselves treasures in heaven, where neither moth nor rust consumes and where thieves do not break in and steal. For where your treasure is, there will your heart be also." Now where do you think your heart was when you were raking those leaves?

2nd Boy: I was thinking about that ten dollars I'd get when I finished!

1st Boy: That's exactly what Jesus was talking about, laying up earthly treasures. That ten dollars could be destroyed and you would never have it again, but Jesus said to lay up treasures in heaven where they can't be destroyed!

2nd Boy: Now I understand! (*Exits running.*)

1st Boy: Where are you going?

2nd Boy (*Offstage*): I'm going back to the lady's house to return the ten dollars and see if I can sweep her driveway for free!

1st Boy: I believe he finally got the picture!

Samson—A Man-Sized Thirst

by Tom deGraaf

Willie: Hey, Cool Charlie, how would you teach a girl to swim?

Cool Charlie: Now you're talking about the Cool Charlie's specialty! You take her little hand in yours, lead her gently down to the water, and say, "Now don't be afraid, sweetie. I wouldn't let anything hurt you."

Willie: Yeah, but the girl is my sister Sally.

Cool Charlie: Oh! Just push her off the dock.

Willie: Yeah.

Dad (*Enters*): Hi, boys.

Willie: Hi, Dad!

Cool Charlie: Hi, Mr. Weekers!

Dad: What'cha doing out here? Isn't it a little hot to be standing around outside?

Cool Charlie: Now that you mention it . . .

Willie: Yeah, it is hot out here, Dad. And me and Cool Charlie was just talkin' about goin' swimmin'.

Dad: Oh, really?

Cool Charlie: Well, sort of . . . We were talking about giving Sally some swimming lessons.

Willie: Hey, I'm getting really thirsty now that I think about it.

Dad: Well, I wouldn't get worked up over trying to teach Sally to swim. Remember last year when your mother and I tried? Sally got a cramp in her face. I mean, she just wasn't cut out to be a swimmer, boys.

Willie: Dad! You're making me more thirsty! I gotta have a drink of water!

Cool Charlie: I could get behind a good drink myself.

Dad: Hey, that reminds me of another great Bible story, boys!

Willie: Aw, Dad! Couldn't we get a drink first and then hear the story?

Dad: Oh, let's be men about this, boys! Besides, it'll make the story more meaningful to you if you wait a second.

Cool Charlie: OK, Mr. Weekers, hit us with the story.

Willie: But make it fast, Dad. I got a real big thirst!

Dad: And that's exactly what my story is about! Remember Samson in the Bible?

Cool Charlie: The strong dude?

Dad: That's the one. This is a little-known story about Samson. He almost died of thirst out on the desert.

Willie: I'm about to die right now . . .

Dad: Well, one day when Samson was out on the desert, he began to notice that the regular water wells in that area were dried up. He went from well to well, only to discover that there was no water to be found! His throat got dry and his tongue began to swell up; and Samson realized he was in trouble, really in trouble. Then he began to think about God. He knew that God would take care of him because they'd gone through many bad and dangerous times before. "God has helped me before," thought Samson, "and he will help me now." So Samson prayed that God would save his life and help him find water.

Suddenly Samson looked over and spotted a hollow spot in the ground. Then, miraculously, he heard the sound of water dripping. There, in the hollow, was water!

Well, Samson knelt down and caught the drips in his hands and drank and drank until his thirst was quenched. He began to feel his strength come back, and he knew he would be strong enough to make it across the desert. God had taken care of Samson; the Bible says, "God careth for you." God had saved Samson's life.

Cool Charlie: That was a cool story, Mr. Weekers! I'd heard of Samson before, but never that story.

Willie: I liked the story too, Dad, but it made me thirstier than I was!

Dad: Well Willie, God careth for you too! I just so happen to have two free coupons for ice-cream cones. Want 'em?

W & C: Does a camel wear a hump? (*Grab coupons and exit.*)

Sally (*Enters*): Where are they going in such a hurry, Dad?

Dad: They're going to get some ice-cream cones, Sally. How was your swimming lesson today, dear?

Sally: Not too good, Dad. First off the pool was empty for cleaning, but the instructor made me do two laps anyway! Then he said I had to practice my diving form for thirty minutes, but I said *no* and came home. I mean it's bad enough that there was no water in the pool, but he said to wear a bathing cap anyway. So I quit.

Dad: It's OK, dear. Wanna hear a story about Samson?

Let's Be Friendly

by W. H. Voorhes and Joey

V: Hi, everyone. How are you today? Joey, say hello to everyone.

J: Hello, everyone.

V: I wonder if anyone of you saw something special at the beach this week?

J: I sure did; I saw the cutest little . . .

V: Joey, remember where you are, now.

J: I saw the cutest little . . . doggie.

V: Oh, OK.

J: I got out of that one, didn't I? (*Looks at audience and winks.*)

V: What did you say, Joey?

J: I said I got something in my eye.

V: Are you sure that's what you said?

J: Let's change the subject.

V: Joey, we'll have to talk about this later on; but I wanted to tell everyone about the big doings at the beach this week. They sunk a great big ship out there for a fishing reef.

J: Do you know what's the greatest ship in the whole world?

V: No, Joey, what is the greatest ship in the whole world?

J: Guess.

V: I can't think what the greatest ship in the whole world is; can anyone else? We give up, Joey; what is the greatest ship in the whole world?

J: Friendship.

V: Hey, that's pretty good. Friendship is a great ship, isn't it?

J: It sure is.

V: That reminds me of a story about friendship in the Bible—about a wee little man.

J: Like me?

V: Well, maybe he wasn't quite as little as you, but he was little, and this wee little man didn't have any friends.

J: That's a sad story. Why didn't he have any friends?

V: Well, because he wasn't very friendly.

J: Oh, didn't he know that to have friends you have to be friendly and be a friend?

V: I guess he didn't know that, Joey.

J: We know, don't we, everyone? We know that we're supposed to be nice to folks and do nice things for them and help them every way we can, don't we? Tell us, did that wee little man ever learn to be friendly?

V: Yes, Joey, Jesus came to his town one day. The little man wanted to see him but couldn't because there were so many people around. So he climbed up into a tree . . .

J: Hey, I know that song that tells about it. Listen:

Zacchaeus was a wee little man
And a wee little man was he.

He climbed up in a sycamore tree
For the Lord he wanted to see . . .

And Jesus said, "Zacchaeus, you come down,
For I'm going to your house today,
I'm going to your house today."

V: Very good, Joey. And Zacchaeus did take Jesus home with him. There Jesus taught him how to be a friend, just like you've learned.

J: Was he nice to folks? And did he help them if he could?

V: Yes, Joey, he became a friend. He wanted to please his new friend, Jesus.

J: That's real good. Hey, everybody, I hope you all try to be friendly with folks so you'll have lots of friends. Especially one in particular, Jesus. He's the best friend of all.

V: That's right, Joey, Jesus is the best friend we can have. But right now, I think it's time for us to go.

J: OK. So long, everyone, talk to you next week.

Noah's Ark

by Jeff Wyers

Mary: Come on, John, and please stop crying.

John: (*Crying*): Why?

Mary: Because you have a pair of lungs that would put an opera star to shame.

John: Why?

Mary: (*To audience*): I only wish I knew. (*To John.*) Now be quiet and I'll tell you a story: Many years ago there was a man named Noah. God told Noah to build an ark for his family and two animals of every kind, one male and one female.

John: Why?

Mary: Because God was mad at the people in the world for being so bad all the time.

John: Why?

Mary: Because God is holy, and all he asked was that they follow him. They wouldn't, so he decided to destroy them and told Noah to get in the boat.

John: Why?

Mary: Because he was going to destroy them—all except Noah, that is, and his family and two animals of every kind. So he told them to get in the boat.

John: Why?

Mary: Because he brought forth a great rain, which lasted forty days and forty nights and caused a big flood, and they floated and floated and finally landed on a mountain.

John: Why?

Mary: So they could remultiply and praise God.

John: Why?

Mary: Because God saved them and put the rainbow in the sky.

John: Why?

Mary: God promised Noah he would never flood the earth again. To show that he meant to keep his promise, he put a rainbow in the sky which could only be seen after a rain.

John: Why?

Mary: Because if it came out before the rain, the colors would all wash off.

John: Ohhh.

Incident Near a Snake Farm

by Tom deGraaf

Willie (*Enters, looks back over shoulder, yells*): Come on, Dad! You and Sally are as slow as turtles on an oil slick.

Sally (*Enters, puffing*): I think I'm gonna die right here in the woods! (*Gasps for air.*)

(**Dad** *enters, keels over on his back, on stage rail, puffing and gasping.*)

Willie (*Crosses, peers into* **Dad**'s *face*): What's the matter, Dad? A little outta shape for this nature trip? I thought you loved hiking!

Sally (*Panting*): You leave Dad alone, Willie. It wasn't his idea to come up here on this stupid hike. I bet we've walked at least ten miles already!

Willie: Would you believe a hundred and fifty yards?

Dad (*Gets up slowly*): Don't worry about me, son. I just stopped to crank up my heart again.

Willie (*Excited*): Ain't this great? Here we are out in the wild country, braving the elements of nature just like the cowboys did. Boy, there's nothing like it.

Sally (*Dismally*): You can say that again. I'd give anything to be sitting down to a nice big pizza and cola right now. This nature stuff is for the birds. Aw, shoot! I gotta go to the bathroom.

Dad: Now, Sally! I know you're tired from hiking, but try to look on the good side.

Sally: Yeah, you're right, Dad. At least I haven't been attacked by some love-crazed mountain man.

Willie: Fat chance!

Dad: Hey, look over there! Isn't that a raccoon by the creek? He's eating a frog for dinner.

Willie: Yuk, Dad! You flipped my stomach.

Sally: And look over there! There's a baby deer! Oh, isn't he cute, Dad? Can I take him home, please? Can I take him home?

Dad: No, dear, I don't . . .

Willie (*Interrupts*): Yeah! Let's catch him and take him home with us! (*Looks down.*) Here's a piece of rope I can use to catch him with! (*Reaches behind stage for what he thinks is a rope. His hand comes up holding a rubber snake.* Hey, this doesn't feel like a rope. (*Looks at it.*)

Sally: Eeeeeagghhh! It's a snake! You picked up a snake, Willie! A snake!

Willie: Eeeeeaaghhggg! (*Throws it behind stage. Both kids run, hug* **Dad**.)

Sally: Oh, Daddy, it was just awful! That snake must have been ten feet long! I wanna go home this instant!

Willie: I had that thing right in my hand, Dad! I could have been bit fifty times! (*Hugging* **Dad**.) It was a great big rattler!

Dad: There, there, kids. It's all over now. The snake is gone and you're both safe with me, OK? Besides, I got a good look at it, and I'm sure it was just a harmless ol' garter snake. (*They let go of* **Dad**.)

Sally: That settles it, Dad. Let's split. I don't mind raccoons or frogs or deers. But I am not going to tolerate being around such a loathsome and despicable creature any longer. And that goes for the snake too.

Willie: Hey, I resent that!

Dad: Do you know what?

W & S: What?

Dad: I just remembered a Bible story about some guys who got attacked by some snakes.

Sally: I don't know if I'm up to any more snake encounters.

Willie: Tell it to us, Dad! I didn't even know there was a snake story in the Bible.

Sally: Don't you remember the snake in the garden with Adam and Evelyn, dummy?

Dad: That's Eve, dear. And anyway, this is a different story.

Sally: OK, Dad. Have it your way. Scare the wits out of me.

Willie: Now you're talkin', Sally. OK, Dad. Let's hear the snake story from the Bible.

Dad: Well, it all begins with Moses and his people, the Israelites. It seems that after they had escaped from being slaves, they wandered out on the desert for many, many years!

Sally: I can sympathize with that. I've been out here thirty-five minutes and I'd give anything to get back to a hamburger joint.

Dad: All of a sudden the people began to complain, Sally. They told Moses they were hot and tired. But they didn't stop there. They began complaining and speaking against God and against Moses. They said they hated the food that God sent them, and they completely forgot about all the times God had taken care of them out in the wilderness. Well, God became angry with the Israelites and sent a bunch of snakes into their camp.

Sally: How frightful!

Willie: What kind of snakes? Were they poisonous?

Dad: Very. Many people were bitten. But they knew why, too. Soon they ran to Moses and said, "We're sorry we spoke against you and against God. Please pray and ask God to take these snakes away from our camp!"

Willie: I would have left 'em there.

Dad: Lucky for the Israelites you're not God, Willie. God told Moses to make a snake out of brass and hang it on a wooden pole. Then, if anyone was bitten by a real snake, he had only to look at the brass snake to be made well again. Well, those real snakes just kept on biting and biting the Israelites. But everyone who would look up to Moses' brass snake on the pole was saved.

Sally: That's what I call creative Medicare.

Dad: No, dear, that's what I call learning a lesson. The Israelites never again talked against God. They were sorry that they had forgotten how he cared for them constantly. They had learned their lesson well.

Willie: That was a neat story, Dad. You know a million of 'em, don't you?

Dad: Yes, Willie, the Bible has many, many stories. The main thing to remember about this one is not the snakes, but the fact that even though the Israelites talked against God and had to be punished, God still loved them enough to save them from the snakes.

Willie: You're right, Dad.

Sally (*Looks down behind the stage, sees something*): Hey, Dad. What does that sign say?

Dad: Where, dear?

Sally: That one stuck on that tree right over there.

Dad: Oh! It says, "Uncle Josh's Snake Farm—enter at your own risk."

S & W (*As they say this line they turn slowly toward each other*): Uncle Josh's Snake Farm? Eeeeaahhh! (*They exit in hysterics.*)

Dad (*Shakes head*): Those kids have got to learn that most snakes are absolutely harmless. I guess they get their fear from their mother. Oh, well, I guess I'll just find myself a walking stick and follow after them. Hee hee hee. (*Reaches down, comes up with rubber snake. Slowly looks at hand, then back at audience, then back at snake. He's frozen, suddenly shrieks, throws snake over shoulder.*)

(*To audience.*) I never thought telling Bible stories would come to this!! (*Exits.*)

The Rebelling Son

by Debbie Smith

Props: *Clothes, Suitcase, Sign "Hawaii," Small Broom*

(*Joe enters carrying several personal belongings.*)

Sally (*Enters and watches* **Joe**): Hey, Joe, what are ya doing?

Joe: I'm packing!

Sally: Packing? Where are you going?

Joe: I'm not sure. All I know is that I'm leaving home. I'm going to run my own life all by myself.

Sally: Joe, are you sure you want to run your own life all by yourself?

Joe: You bet I am. I'm tired of everybody telling me what to do. I'm gonna take all my things and just do what I want to do and have a good time.

Sally: But what will you do if you run out of money, friends, and things to do?

Joe: I don't want to think about that now. I just want to have a good time.

Sally: I know of someone else who didn't think about that either.

Joe: Where is he now? Maybe he and I could get together and have some fun.

Sally: Well, I don't know his name, but it's someone Jesus talked about in the Bible.

Joe: Sally, if you must tell me this story, would you please hurry so I can get going. I've got places to go and people to see!

Sally: Joe, I want you to listen and watch!

(**Sally** *tells story of the prodigal son while other puppets act it out.*) A man had two sons.

1: I'm number 1.

2: I'm number 2.

Sally: One day the younger son told his father:

2: Hey, Dad, I want my share of things so I can go do my own thing.

Sally: The father let the son go on his own.

—The son packed all his belongings . . .

(*Belongings thrown up in the air.*)

—and traveled to a distant land.

(*Sign—Hawaii*)

—There the son partied and partied, and partied some more.

Joe: Now that's the life!

Sally: Until all his money was gone.

—About this time a famine swept across the land.

(*Broom sweeps slowly across the stage.*)

—And he began to starve.

(**2** *faints.*)

—He saw a local farmer and begged him,

2: Oh please, Mr. Local Farmer. I need a job. I'm starving; I'll do anything you say.

Farmer: Well, son, with this famine coming up, there just ain't much to do around these parts. Hm . . . you could feed my pigs for me. (*Pig call—sounds.*)

Sally: The boy became so hungry that even the pods that he was feeding the pigs looked good to him.

Joe: Yuk! He must have been awfully hungry.

Sally: Yes, he was, Joe, and no one would give him anything. When he finally came to his senses, he said to himself:

2: Self, back at home even my dad's hired men have food to eat, and even some left over. Here I am starving. I see now that I was wrong. I will go back to my dad and ask his forgiveness.

Sally: So he returned home and before he even got home, his father saw him coming and ran to meet him. The son said to his father (**Father** *enters*):

2: Dad, I'm really sorry. I just ruined everything. I know I'm not worthy to even be called your son. Could I work for you as your servant?

Father: Son, I love you. I'm so glad you have come home.

Let's celebrate your coming with a great party, for once my son left me, but now he has returned.

Joe: That father sure loved his son.

Sally: Well, that's how much God loves us. God waits for us to come to him because he loves us.

Joe: Why would anyone want to leave someone who loves him that much?

Sally: Have you forgotten? You were ready to leave, weren't you?

Joe: Oh—oh—I guess I was.

Sally: God loves you; he made you; and he knows what is best for you.

Joe: But how do I face him when I acted like he wasn't even there?

Sally: Joe, God loved us so much that he sent his Son, Jesus, to die for us. If we trust in Jesus, then we never have to be away from God. Hey, Joe, you still wanna leave?

Joe: I don't think so. I'll stick around here now that I know someone really loves me.

Sally: That's great! I would have missed you, too!

How to Be a Witness Without Being Weird

by Sally Whittington

1 (*With skateboard*): Boy, my new skateboard is so neat! I'm so glad I finally got one! (*Kisses it.*) I just know I'm going to be good at this—it looks so easy—I'll just hop right on and take a ride. Oh. OOHH! Wooah! Eyyyy! (*Crash, slam, bang, etc.*) Moan. Moan! Ohh! Pain! My finger. My finger! I skinned my poor little finger! Oh! No! It's going to bleed! I just know it's going to bleed! *HELP!*

2 (*Approaching cautiously, carrying Bible and hat*): Well, my goodness. What's all this?

1 (*Holding back tears*): Well, you see, I had this terrible accident, and I need *help!*

2: Well, my goodness! Don't you know what day this is? It's Sunday! And don't you know what time it is? It's 9:43½! If I help you, I'll be late for Sunday School! It was very thoughtless of you to have your "terrible accident" only one block from the church! You're going to tie up traffic and make everybody late for Sunday School! My goodness . . . (*Exits, shaking head.*)

3 (*Approaches, counting to self*): 12-13-14-15—17! Seventeen of these tracts I've given out today. That's 17 people I've won to the Lord! I never knew soul-winning was so easy—why, there's nothing to it—just hand 'em a tract, say "God bless you," and . . . (*Sees* 1) Well, what's this?

1: It's a terrible accident, that's what it is, and I need *help!*

3: Oh! Well, I know just what you need! Here. Have a tract. (*Hands him tract.*)

1 (*Looks at tract*): Why, thank you! What does it say?

3 (*Briskly*): How should I know? I haven't read it! I'm already a Christian!

1 (*Hesitantly*): Well—how do I use it?

3: Maybe you could use it as a bandage for your hurt finger. (*Exits, speaking.*) Let's see, 14, 15, 16—18! That's 18 people I've won to the Lord today. Boy, I'll bet God's really proud of me! Oh (*Turns back to* 1), God bless you! (*Exits.*)

4 (*Enters humming, with big sign—REPENT*): Oh, what happened to you?

1 (*Holding back tears*): Well, you see, I had this terrible accident, and I hurt my finger, and I need *help!*

4: Read the sign.

1: What sign? Oh, no! My vision must be getting blurred! I'm going into shock! (*Starts weaving.*) Help!

4: Repent!

1 (*Cowering behind skateboard*): What?

4 (*Loudly and judgmentally, stepping closer during delivery until he is towering over* 1): For all have sinned and come short of the glory of God—unless you repent you will all likewise perish—be not deceived, God is not mocked, for what so ever a man soweth, that also shall he reap!

There! What do you think about that?

1 (*Weakly*): But . . . but . . . didn't I hear somewhere that God loves me, even though I am a sinner?

4: I never saw that in my Bible! (*Walks away, turns to deliver one more scathing rebuke.*) REPENT! (*Exits.*)

5 (*Enters, reading aloud Matt. 25:35-40*): Wow! What a neat Scripture! Just think! When we serve others, we're serving God. How neat! (*Impatiently.*) What are you doin' lying on the ground?!

1 (*Panting*): Terrible accident . . . Sinking fast . . . *Help!*

5: Get this skateboard out of my way! I can't get through— and I'm looking for someone to help! (*Walks by 1, reading with much feeling.*) I was hungry and you . . .

6 (*Enters*): Oh! What happened to you? It looks like a terrible accident . . .

1: Well, it's not! It's a terrible acci— Oh, thank goodness! *Help* has finally arrived!

6: Here, let's see. Where are you hurt? Oh, it's your finger. It looks like it might bleed. You just relax, now, and I'll clean your finger with my handkerchief. Is this a new skateboard? It's really a nice one. I fell off mine the first time I rode it and skinned my nose.

1 (*Sarcastically*): Oh. Is that what happened to it?

6: Yep. There now. You've had quite an experience. My house is just down the street; why don't you come home with me and rest for a while? My mom will fix us milk and cookies, and maybe we can get to be friends. Say, speaking of friends, I'd like to tell you about my very best friend. His name is Jesus, and he loves me so much that he was willing to die in my place! Do you have a friend like that?

1 (*Showing interest*): Why, no, I don't . . .

6: Well, Jesus wants to be your friend too. Let me tell you how you can get to know him . . . (*Both exit.*)

When I Am Afraid

by Tom deGraaf

Scene: *A campfire.*

Dad (*Prodding campfire with stick;* **Willie, Cool Charlie** *enter*): Hi, boys. Did you get our tent up OK? It's very important to have a good tent made when you're out in the woods camping.

Cool Charlie: Sure, Mr. Weekers. I got the tent up all by myself. (*Glares at* **Willie,** *who lowers head, embarrassed.*)

Dad: Didn't you help Cool Charlie, Willie?

Cool Charlie: He sure didn't, Mr. Weekers. He got scared of a chipmunk and zipped himself shut in your sleeping bag. He didn't come out for an hour!

Willie: Sorry, Dad . . . But that chipmunk gritted his teeth at me, and . . .

Dad: Never mind. It's OK. Hey, isn't this just great being out here in the forest? Just smell those pine trees! (*Sniffs.*) What's that? (*Sniffs again.*) What's that I smell? (*Sniffs.*)

Cool Charlie: It's skunk perfume. Willie got it while he was getting water out of the creek. He tripped over a skunk, and it unloaded on Willie's foot. PU!

Dad: Well, why don't you go hang your boots in a tree to air out and then come back? We'll all sit around the campfire and tell stories. How's that sound?

Cool Charlie: Great idea, Mr. Weekers! A campfire story!

Willie: Yeah! That sounds like fun, Dad!

Dad: OK. You guys hurry it up and get back here.

W & C: See you in a minute! (*Exit.*)

Cool Charlie (*Reenters, looking to see if* **Willie** *has fol-*lowed him. To **Dad**): Pssssst!

Dad (*Startled*): OH! You scared me, Cool Charlie! I thought you went to help Willie hang up his stinky shoes.

Cool Charlie: I just had to talk to you when Willie wasn't around, Mr. Weekers.

Dad: Why? Is there something wrong with Willie?

Cool Charlie: He's afraid of being out here, Mr. Weekers. He didn't want to tell you about it, but he's really afraid to be out here in the forest. Do you know that he almost went to pieces when he saw that chipmunk today?

Dad: Well . . . yes, he said he jumped into my sleeping bag.

Cool Charlie: Yeah, but did he tell you that your sleeping bag was still in the car, still rolled up?

Dad: Hmmm . . . He must have been frightened. Well, I had no idea, Cool Charlie. I'll have a little talk with him when he comes back. (*Thinks of something, puts hand to head.*) Are you thinking what I'm thinking?

Cool Charlie: Oh, no! You mean that Willie is out there hanging up his stinky shoes by himself?

Willie (*Yells*): Cool Charlie, where are you? Aaarrrgggh! (*Enters, knocks campfire down, grabs* **Dad.**)

Dad: Hey . . . hey now! What's the matter, son?

Cool Charlie: He knocked the campfire all to pieces! (*Puts it back in place.*)

Willie (*Feeling foolish*): Uh . . . excuse me, Dad. I must have gone berserk there for a minute. I couldn't find Cool Charlie and I got scared . . . I mean, I got worried about him.

Dad: Sure you did, son. And Cool Charlie got a little scared too, didn't you, Cool Charlie?

Cool Charlie: Me? Scared? You gotta be . . . Oh . . . Yeah, Mr. Weekers, I got a little . . . (*Hates to say it.*) scared too.

Dad: Thank you, Cool Charlie.

Willie: Really? Wow, I thought Cool Charlie never was afraid! (**Cool** *bites his fist to keep silent.*)

Dad: Oh, we all get afraid sometimes, Willie. And I'm going to tell you guys a story about what to do when you do get afraid. Now let's get this fire straight and get comfy and I'll begin.

Willie: Dad, are you afraid of lizards?

Dad: No, son. They're perfectly delightful little creatures. Why do you ask?

Willie (*Looks down*): Well, I just saw a great big one zip up your pants leg.

> (**Dad** *looks down, jumps, yells tries to shake out lizard. Knocks campfire down again.*)

Cool Charlie: Hey, that was outa sight, Mr. Weekers! You can really boogie when you want to!

Willie: Terrific, Dad!

Dad (*Regains composure*): Never mind that, boys. Now, where were we?

Willie: You were going to tell us about being afraid.

Dad: Oh, yes. Well . . . just a minute. Cool Charlie, go get the campfire again. (*He gets it, puts it back.*) Now, there once was an old man named Jesse, who had a very large family. One of his children, the youngest one, was named David. Old Jesse loved his young son David very much and wanted to teach him how to be brave.

Willie: Why's that?

Dad: Well, back in those days the people had life a lot tougher than we do today, and Jesse wanted his young son David to be able to take care of himself. Jesse told David stories about God and about how he watched over little children. He told David that if ever he was afraid, he should remember that God loved him and was watching over him.

Willie: He was sure watching over me when that chipmunk attacked!

Dad: Uh, yeah . . . Well, Jesse sent David out onto the hillside to watch over his sheep. For many days at a time,

David would stay out there and sleep out there with the flock of sheep. David was their protector.

Cool Charlie: Not what you'd call an exciting line of work.

Dad: Well, not always. Sometimes David was very lonely out there, and sometimes he was afraid. At night he would sit around the campfire by himself and make up little songs and verses, and they would help him not be so lonely or afraid.

Willie: What's to be afraid of? A few sheep?

Dad: Oh, there were a lot of things to be afraid of. Once a lion came to eat the sheep, and David had to kill it. He killed that lion all by himself!

Cool Charlie: And Willie was afraid of a chipmunk! A haw haw!

Dad: OK, Cool Charlie. And another time a terrible bear came, and David bravely killed it too. David had a little song that he had written that helped him not to be afraid. It's a song that's in our Bible. Would you like to hear it?

Willie: Yeah! Maybe it'll help me not to be afraid.

Dad: It goes like this: "What time I am afraid, I will put my trust in thee." That means David would put his trust in God, and God would help him not to be afraid. David never forgot that song or how God helped him kill the lion and the bear. David knew that God would watch over him always.

Willie: That's great, Dad. Will you repeat that song?

Dad: OK, son. (*Repeats it.*) Well, boys, I guess it's time to get in our sleeping bags for the night. You won't be afraid, will you, Willie?

Willie: Not after learning that song.

Dad: Good! And in the morning we'll all hike to the lake and get some big old brown trout!

Cool Charlie: Right on!

Willie: All right!

Dad: Good. I'm proud of you boys for being so brave. Now let's get some sleep! (*They start off.*) Oh, Cool Charlie, get the campfire, will you? We don't want to start a forest fire. (**Dad** *and* **Willie** *exit.* **Cool Charlie** *follows, carrying campfire.*)

Harry the Skeptic

by Walter Norvell

(*This skit was written to go along with a sermon based on references from Jonah. It should be used early in the service. The pastor [or another real person] should speak the opening lines so as not to let on that a puppet is about to appear. Surprise is an important element.*)

Pastor: Last week I met a young man. He seemed to be

quite an interesting young man, but something of a skeptic. In fact, he *was* a skeptic. As the conversation led to religion, he just couldn't accept the things I had to say. Well, to make a long story short, I gave Harry a Bible, asked him to read my sermon reference in advance, and invited him to church. He said he'd come today . . . but I don't see him . . . I guess . . .

Harry: Hm . . . hm . . . Oh, hi there, Rev. Is this the place?

Pastor: Yes, Harry. Glad you could make it. Did you read the reference I told you about?

Harry: Yea . . . sure. (*Mood changes.*) Rev., there's something fishy about that story. It's the biggest whale of a tale I've ever heard. Did you expect me to believe it?

Pastor: You, Harry? No, I *never* expected *you* to believe it. What else, if anything, did you think of the story?

Harry: Well, besides that big, unbelievable fish, this guy Jonah was a little hard to swallow, too.

Pastor: Why?

Harry: First of all, I thought all these Bible characters were supposed to be superhuman or something. Bible people were supposed to be good all the time—never did anything wrong—always doing just what God told them. This Jonah fellow was just too normal. Like us!

Pastor: Harry, you might be a skeptic, but at least you're a perceptive one. Jonah was like us. I guess he was a "nominal Jew." You read how he ran from God and how God used dangers and perils to set Jonah in the right direction. Then, when things didn't go Jonah's way again, he just gave up, sat down, and pouted about it. But God was always with him.

Harry: Yea . . . and that's another thing. I thought that if you got out of line God just struck you with lightning or gave you leprosy or got rid of you somehow.

Pastor: Harry, I think Jonah's case shows that God loves his people. He wants us to have his blessings and do his will. Whether we are seeking God or running from him, God is always seeking us with his love.

Harry: I guess this story makes more sense now. Do you think Jonah ever understood about God's love?

Pastor: Yes, I think he began to understand after he changed his point of view. After he got things done in Nineveh, where God wanted him, he could see a little better than when he was running away from God toward Joppa.

Harry: Yea, Rev. I guess it all depends on where you're going.

Pastor: That's right. Harry—I think you're going in the right direction, too.

Harry: Yea? . . . Well, I think I'll find a seat. Go on with the service. I want to hear what else you have to say.

Pastor: OK, Harry.

Harry: Oh yeah, I remember something else about the story. Man, this would make a great movie!

Pastor: That's great! All about God's love for us.

Harry: No! No! About a big fish that goes around eating everybody. Boy! It'd make a million dollars. I can see it now. Call it "Teeth" . . . terrorizes a seashore community . . . what an idea! (*Wanders off in his new dream.*)

Penelope Prays

by Judy Simmons

Penelope Pharisee: Hello, everyone. I am Penelope Pharisee. I have come to the church today to pray. I am going to stand outside so you can see me better. (*Looks at watch.*) Well, I guess I am ready to begin. Is everyone listening?

(*Looks up toward heaven—doesn't close eyes. Stretches arms out and begins to pray in a fairly loud voice.*)

Lord, I know you are glad to hear from me. I have been so busy today doing your work. You just wouldn't believe how difficult it is to do good deeds. But I have been working steadily. I am sure you will have a special reward waiting for me when I arrive in heaven. Lord, today I did many good works in your name. I visited Mary Jones at home. She wasn't terribly sick, but I thought it my Christian duty to go and see her. I told her she shouldn't get out of the house until she could wash her hair—she really looked a fright, Lord. But I stood it somehow. You know, her house was terrible. But I tore into that lazy daughter of hers. By

the time I left Mary had crawled back into the bed and her daughter was crying—the baby's ear was infected too. I told Mary that's what happened when you neglected your housework. I hope she'll remember that piece of advice when she gets well.

(**Susan Sinner** *enters. She bows down, prays softly.*)

Susan Sinner: Father, have mercy on me. I am a sinner. Wash me and cleanse me, O Lord, and . . .

Penelope: Lord, I hear something. I'm afraid someone is trying to cut in on my conversation. (*Looks toward* **Susan.**) Oh, good grief, it's Susan Sinner! She's got some nerve. Hmmmph!

Lord, don't listen to her right now. I was here first! Honestly, I can't believe anyone could pray in that fashion. Why, I couldn't even breathe all curled up like that! Lord, are you listening to her?

Susan: Father, I have sinned and need your forgiveness. I am not worthy to be called your child . . .

Penelope: Lord, I can guarantee that! She is not worthy to be one of yours. Now, if you don't mind, let's get back to the conversation we were having. (*Speaks louder to cover up* **Susan's** *voice.*)

Lord, I made my special casserole and took it to the meeting our Woman's Missionary Union was sponsoring. I spent *all* morning there. I was supposed to bring sandwiches, but I just knew those people would rather have tuna casserole. And they did love it. Boy, it really made the other women jealous, though. Everyone was clustering around me, trying to get some of my casserole before it disappeared. But, Lord, the way I see it, those women should have known better than to bring sandwiches. Anyone knows people would rather have a hot meal than sandwiches any old day. At any rate, if they are jealous, that's their problem, as I see it!

Susan: Thank you, Lord, for forgiving me. I will go and try to do better now. (*Exits.*)

Penelope: Lord, I just have to tell you this. Just in case you didn't notice, that woman prayed an awfully short prayer. (*Looks at watch.*) I've been going on for nearly a half-hour. And I'm almost positive her prayer was only six minutes long!

Well, I guess it's time for me to go now, too, Lord. I just have one more thing to add.

Lord, you know how tough it is to do good deeds. I did all these many works today and not one person said thank you. In fact, some of them, like Mary Jones and her daughter, acted downright ungrateful. At least when you healed those ten lepers, one of them did come back to thank you. Lord, how long before I get my reward?

If You Ask in Faith

by Tom deGraaf

(**Willie** *and* **Sally** *enter, carrying Sunday School quarterlies.* **Willie** *has a tie on, and* **Sally** *is wearing a hat.*)

Willie: I just can't believe it, Sally.

Sally: Me either. Who'd even think that Cool Charlie would get so sick he'd have to go to the hospital?

Willie: Oh, man, I hope he makes it!

Sally: Me too. He's really my best friend other than Silvia.

Willie: He's also your only friend other than Silvia.

Sally (*Ignoring remark*): Do you remember what Mrs. Frumpmire said in Sunday School today about praying?

Willie: Yeah, I think she said we should close our eyes and not pinch.

Sally (*Irritated*): No! Not that. I mean, remember the part about if we pray in faith God will answer us?

Willie (*Seriously*): Do you mean that if we just pray in faith, God will answer all our prayers?

Sally: That's what Mrs. Frumpmire said. Maybe we should pray that Cool Charlie will not get any worse sick. I've got faith!

Willie: Why don't we pray that he gets out of the hospital, completely well in two weeks? I've got faith too, you know!

Sally (*Excited at the prospects*): Hey, why not pray that he gets out in one week? I've got faith.

Willie (*Excited too*): Well, I've got even more! How 'bout he gets out day after tomorrow?

Sally: Let's pray that he gets out in time for Training Union tonight! I've got faith!

Willie: Right on, Sally! I didn't even know we had this much faith! (*They start praying. Suddenly* **Willie** *stops, looks straight ahead, has an idea, nudges* **Sally**.)

Willie: Pssst. Hey, Sally.

Sally (*Annoyed*): Willieeee . . . Can't you see that I'm praying as hard as I can for Cool Charlie to get well? Buzz off.

Willie: But Sally . . . If we pray this hard for Cool and he gets well like Mrs. Frumpmire says, why don't we pray and ask for a few things for ourselves too?

Sally (*Hesitant*): Well, she did say that if we asked in faith God would answer. (*Excited.*) Hey, that's a brilliant idea! I've got faith that God will give me a new flex-o-skateboard!

Willie: And I've got faith that he'll give me a new ten-speed!

(*They start praying frantically for everything they can think of—skateboard, bicycles, puka shells, water skis, backpacks, and so forth.*)

Dad (*Enters wearing tie, carrying Bible, stops, listens to his kids for a moment*): Uh, Willie, Sally? (*They stop praying.*)

Sally (*Excited*): Oh, Dad! It's so wonderful! Isn't it wonderful, Willie?

Willie: It's wonderful, Dad! Just great! Outta sight!

Dad: It sounds like you're rehearsing for Christmas. What's going on here?

Sally: Well, Cool Charlie is in the hospital and . . .

Dad (*Interrupts*): Cool Charlie is in the hospital?

Willie: Yeah, Dad. He's real sick too!

Dad: What's the matter with him?

Sally: Well, he decided to go to one of those new health clubs to build up his arms. Unfortunately, it was more than just his arms that needed working on.

Willie: The health club manager said it was the first time he ever saw anyone go from push-ups to intensive care.

Dad: But you guys weren't praying for Cool Charlie just now. You were asking for stuff you want.

Sally: And that's the neat part, Dad! Willie and I just found out how to get everything we want! All we have to do is pray . . . with faith!

Willie: That's right! Mrs. Frumpmire said that whatever we ask for in faith, we can get.

Sally: And Willie and I suddenly found out how much faith we've got! Plenty!

Dad (*Scratches head in thought*): Hmmmm . . . (*Pauses.*)

Sally (*Looks at Dad*): What's wrong, Dad? Are you trying to think of some stuff you and Mom want?

Willie: How 'bout a new house, or a swimming pool?

Dad: I'm afraid that you kids didn't understand what Mrs. Frumpmire said today.

Sally: Sure we did, Dad. She said, and I quote from Matthew 21:22, "Whatever you ask in prayer, you shall receive, if you have faith." Me and Willie got faith, so we're askin'.

Dad: You're right about needing faith to pray, Sal, but do you know what faith really is?

Sally: Sure, Dad. It's real hard wishing.

Dad: And what do you think faith is, Willie?

Willie: I'll go along with Sally—It's just good hard wishing and hoping.

Dad: Kids, come over here. God only asks us to do three main things as Christians: To glorify him, to grow in Christlikeness, and to lead other people to be saved. Now those three things are what our prayers should be about. They are the things that make up our prayers of faith to God.

Sally: You mean wishing and hoping real hard isn't praying in faith?

Dad: No, Sally. When you pray to God in faith, that means you're praying for something that will glorify God, or for help to be more like Jesus, or that someone will be saved.

Willie: But what about praying for Cool Charlie to get well?

Dad: That is a prayer of faith because healing is to the glory of God, in the eyes of Christians.

Sally: I guess my asking for a skateboard isn't a good idea, huh?

Dad: Well, Sally, God does want us to be happy; and he knows what we need and don't need. So you can pray for whatever you want, if you feel that God wants you to have it. But remember, real prayers are based on our faith that God will be glorified, or that we will grow to be more like Jesus, or that someone will be saved.

Sally: I think I understand now, Dad.

Dad: Good, dear. I'm proud of you.

Willie: I understand too, Dad! God takes care of the important and serious stuff.

Dad: Right!

Willie: And you take care of the skateboards and ten-speeds!

(**Dad** *is bewildered.*)

Sally: Far out, Dad! (*Hugs him.*) You're so smart, Dad! You know everything. I love you! (*Kisses* **Dad,** *who is staring at audience, bewildered.*)

Willie: Come on, Sally! Let's go down to the toy store and pick out our stuff! (*They exit.*)

Dad (*Stares at audience*): How do I get myself into these situations? Sometimes I think those kids understand better than I do. (*Exits, looking into Bible.*)

Section III

SEASONAL

A Christmas Experience

by J. Michael Hensley

(**Puppet** *enters, singing "O Christmas Tree," and walks over to admire his tree*).

WOW! Christmas is here already! Isn't this tree simply beautiful? I really love Christmas! Though it seems like only yesterday I was swimming and playing softball in the *hot* sunshine. But I can really tell it's almost Christmas. That air is really cold! (*Whew!*)

Now where is my stocking? (*Looking around.*) Gotta hang my stocking! If I don't, Santa might pass on by thinking I was bad or that I don't want anything. Can't let that happen! Where is it? Ha, Ha! I was a pretty good ole boy this year, except for _____ and _____ , and then there was _____ . Oh well, I'd rather not think about those times. *Hee, Hee!* (*Looks down behind curtain.*) There's my stocking down there. Now how did it get down there? Oh, well. (*Exits to get stocking and reenters, singing "Here Comes Santa Claus." As he sings, he hangs stocking over edge of stage nearest tree.*)

There! Now that does it! Just right! Santa won't miss me now! Only seven days left until Christmas. Boy, I can't wait! I sure hope Santa brings everything I asked for. Let's see, there was an electric train set, a Bionic man and woman, new tennis shoes, and a warm-up suit so I can play basketball in the church's Family Life Center, a poster of Farrah Fawcett-Majors, a James Taylor album, and a real Pontiac Firebird Trans Am or Camaro Z-28, whichever Santa can get. I'm not particular! Man, that'll be great! Super fantastic! (*Walks to opposite end of stage from Christmas tree.*)

Hey, look out there at all those stars. They sure are bright, but over there is one that will almost blind a person. WOW! It almost lights up all outside! I bet it's like the star the Wise Men followed so many years ago. Yeah, really makes you stop and think what Christmas is all about. The Christ child, God's Son, coming into the world because of his unending love for me. (*Pauses and looks for a moment, then turns and walks back to the Christmas tree, looking at the tree for a moment.*) Man, that's heavy stuff! Just think, the Christ child came into the world for *me* and everyone like me and different from me! (*Pauses as if thinking, then exits singing "Silent Night."*)

'Tis the Season to Be . . .

by Mary Lou Serratt

(**Props:** a backdrop of black sky with silver stars; confetti snowflakes—*Use a hand dryer from below to make it "snow."*)

(**Joey, Kate,** *and Carolers are heard singing "Deck The Halls." They get louder as they enter. A small puppet is at end of the stage, listening.* **Joey** *and* **Kate** *bump into him, stopping their progress.*)

Joey: Hey, wait, you guys! (*They stop singing.*) There's someone in our way. (*To* **Stranger.**) Why don't you move off the sidewalk and get out of the way? We're carolers.

Kate: Yeah, and Christmas carolers always have the right of way during Christmas week!

Stranger: Oh, sorry . . . I only now moved here from . . . (*Pausing.*) from afar off. We never had carolers there. You sound happy and of cheer . . . that made me listen and I did not move.

Joey: Yeah, well, OK. But we gotta go or we'll be late for the party at the church.

Kate: Right! (*Other carolers nod, talk.*) And then we won't have time to put up the manger scene.

Stranger: Please . . . what is "manger"?

Joey: Oh, c'mon, you know, manger, shepherds, Wise Men, Jesus—all those Christmas things.

Kate (*Interrupting*): Let's go, Joey.

Stranger: I know Christmas . . . Saint Nicholas . . . uh . . . Sante Clas. (*Carolers laugh.*) But who is this manger?

Joey: Man, you can't be for real! See . . .

Kate (*Interrupting*): Joey! The hot chocolate will be cold! (*The carolers chime in with "yeah, let's go" . . . "hurry up" . . . and so on.*)

Joey: Well (*To carolers*), yeah. (*To Stranger.*) You better ask somebody to straighten you out about Christmas, fellow.

Stranger: But I don't know somebody!

Kate and Carolers: Joey . . . let's go . . . (*and so forth*).

Joey (*Looks at Stranger, then at friends*): Right . . . Move over, fellow. (*To carolers.*) OK, guys, let's start over.

(*Stranger moves to back of stage as carolers pass in front and exit, singing loudly.*).

All Carolers: "Deck the halls with boughs of holly, fa la la la la, la la la la . . . 'Tis the season to be jolly, Fa (*Starts to fade out.*) la la la la, La la la la . . ."

Stranger (*Waits until all is quiet . . . moves to front of stage, looks after carolers, then at audience*): 'Tis the season to be confused—and lonely. (*Exits slowly.*)

Christmas Joy

by Philip R. McCraw

(*In background, carolers are heard singing "O Come All Ye Faithful."*)

Flucy Lucy (*Enters*): "O Come All Ye Faithful" indeed! If I had to come or go one more time, I think I'd croak. I'm not dreaming of a white Christmas, either—I just want to be dreaming, period. I haven't slept good in a week, trying to get all the details together. Stuff to get, what to cook, who gets what gift—

Wild Willie (*Rushes up, yelling painfully, and wiggling*): Yiii-hyyy! Boy, Lucy, am I glad to see you.

Lucy: My goodness, are you that excited about Christmas?

Willie: Gosh, no! What's got me excited right now is these cedar splinters sticking in my backside. Yii-ouch ohh! And I'm glad to see you 'cause I hope you will—ouch—pull them out. (*He bends over the front of the stage.*)

Lucy (*Laughing cruelly*): Ha Ha—they say 'tis the season to be jolly. I think this is going to be fun. How about if I just rubbed them in a little?

Willie (*Raises up sharply*): No! Ou-u-u. Ohh! *Please*, Lucy, give me a break.

Lucy (*Still chuckling*): OK, I'd really be delighted. But this is gonna hurt you a whole lot more than it's gonna hurt me.

Willie (*Leaning over, moaning*): Just do it, OK?

Lucy: (*Behind Willie*): Oh, here's one. (*She yanks; Willie screams.*) Here's a nice one (*Repeat*). And here's one. (*Willie screams, then sighs in relief.*)

Willie: Thanks.

Lucy: How do you spell relief? (*Chuckles.*) Well, Willie, what have you been up to besides sitting on Christmas trees? (*Hee, hee, hee.*)

Willie: I wasn't sitting on it; I was falling on it while trying to decorate the silly thing. I tripped over Uncle Leonard's Christmas present and zappo! Now my tree's in a complete mess. I may even have to buy another one; and besides, I'm tired of decorating. This decorating is a pain in the neck!

Lucy: In your case, the pain is elsewhere. (*Chuckling.*)

Willie (*Glaring at her*): You think it's funny, don't you? Well . . . (*Sniff, sniff*). Don't I smell something burning?

Lucy (*Screaming*): My cake! (*Exits.*)

Willie (*Sarcastically*): As you said, 'tis the season to be jolly. (*Ha, ha.*)

Lucy (*Enters*): Well, it's ruined. I've had Christmas till I'm sick of the thought. I wish it was over.

Willie: Well, I've had Christmas till I'm broke. And yesterday, my overused bank-card crumpled into pieces. The smart-aleck clerk said, "Ho, ho, ho." I told her to stick it in her ear.

Lucy: Yeah, that's nothing; my feet are all swollen. Not only did I walk the length of the mall twice yesterday, but people also kept stepping on them; the place was so crowded. And this one little kid kicked me because he wanted my candy cane!

Willie: Well, that's not so tough—at least *you* didn't fall into a cedar tree!

Lucy: Why do we do this every year?

Willie: I don't. First time I ever fell into a cedar tree. And, believe me! I do not plan to make it a habit.

Lucy: No, you know what I mean! We destroy ourselves every year, and why? Just to please everybody, that's why. Always trying to give a bigger gift to someone than the one given last year. Inviting everybody over for parties and stuff.

Willie: Yeah, we're so busy and tired from being joyful that we are miserable. Ho, ho, ho, and pass me my nerve pills.

Lucy: But why don't we just stop all this nonsense?

Susie Dog (*Enters with Egbert*): I heard that, and Christmas is not nonsense. It is a time for us to really show people that we love them. It's a time for everybody to remember love. And, oh, it's really a time for the children. It's a happy time. I wish adults wouldn't gripe about it so much. They could enjoy Christmas, too.

Egbert: Yes, that's true. Also, Christmas is a time to remember the Christ child. Our God sent his only Son into our world. That's the real celebration of Christmas—it's

remembering that Jesus Christ is born. Oh, how very much that means. A Savior has come to bring us the peace on earth that passes all understanding. Let us not forget that.

Lucy: You know, you are right. I must ask God to forgive me for my bad attitude. That's really all that is wrong—it's my attitude.

Willie: Yes, plus we forget how really dynamic this birth was. This season is one of joyous celebration, and I was neglecting that.

Egbert: Let's think about the specialness of this season as we hear the Christmas story from God's Word. (**Narrator** *or* **puppets** *read Christmas story.*)

Sharing with Others

by Shirley Martin

(**Mary** *snores.*)

Sarah (*Enters, goes over, pushes her*): Get up! Christmas is almost here and we have work to do.

(**Mary** *turns over, continues to snore.*)

Sarah: Mary! You get up. (*Pushes her again.*)

Mary (*Voice muffled*): Go away.

Sarah: Get up, Mary. We have work to do.

Mary: Work? You can forget me. (*Snores.*)

Sarah: Get up, Mary. You have to get up. (**Mary** *snores.*) I know. I will turn on the radio. That will wake her up. (*Exits. Loud music is heard in background. Enters again.*) Still not up? I said, Get up!

Mary: Let me sleep.

Sarah: You can't. It is almost Christmas.

Mary: You take care of it.

Sarah: Mary, get up. You know we have to meet at the church to gather food for those who do not have any.

Mary: You like to do things like that. I like to sleep.

Sarah: You are even too lazy to eat. You have already slept through breakfast. Now get up.

Mary: Call me when it is time to open the presents.

Sarah (*Yells*): Mary! I'll give you one more chance. Get up!

Mary: No! (*Turns, snores again.*)

Sarah: I know. I will tickle her. (*Tickles her.*) I told you to

get up.

Mary (*Laughing*): OK, I am up. Now leave me alone.

Sarah: There are people out there who do not have enough to eat; and you don't care enough to share with them?

Mary: Look, on Christmas I get presents; and that is all I care about.

Sarah: Christmas is for giving, not getting.

Mary: You give. I will get.

Sarah: If I do not give, you will not get anything.

Mary: You mean I won't get anything for Christmas?

Sarah: That could be.

Mary: You will not give me a present?

Sarah: Maybe.

Mary: But I want a present.

Sarah: Sure you do.

Mary: Please give me a present so I can have Christmas.

Sarah: There are people out there who don't have anything. If someone doesn't give to them, they won't have any Christmas. Now you stay here if you want to, but I am going to gather food to send to those who do not have any. I am going to give to them. I am going to enjoy a Merry Christmas even without you.

Mary: I see what you mean. I will help you.

Sarah: Come on then. (*Both exit.*)

Incident at the Christmas Tree Lot

by Tom deGraaf

(**Willie** *and* **Sally** *enter excited in hats, coats, mufflers, and so forth.*)

Sally: Oh, isn't this exciting, Willie! I just love picking out a Christmas tree! (*Looks around slowly.*) Oh, they're all so lovely! There's hundreds of 'em!

Willie: Yeah, this is cool! . . . Hey, where's Dad?

Sally: I think he stayed at the fire in that trash can by the flocking booth.

Willie: Well, I want him to help us pick out a tree! I'm going to get him. (*Starts to exit, but* **Sally** *grabs him.*)

Sally: Wait a minute, reindeer breath. Dad couldn't find his long undies, so just let him stay by the fire. We can pick out the tree by ourselves.

Willie: Hey, yeah! Let's get a fifteen-footer this year!

Sally: We've only got an eight-foot ceiling in the house.

Willie: Well, let's get a great big thick tree, then!

Sally: The cat got lost in the last one, remember?

Willie: Then let's get a thin one and flock it!

Sally: Mom says she can't get the flock off the carpet.

Willie (*Irritated*): So what are you saying, Sally—that we just bring home a convenient "creeping Charlie" or something? How am I gonna choose a tree with all your negative poo-pahs?

Sally (*Grabs him*): And how would you like a "positive" poo-pah right in the lip?

Dad (*Enters cold*): OK, OK. Sally, let go of your brother. (*She does, and he falls down behind stage.*) I knew I should have stayed by the fire.

Sally (*Excited*): Oh, Daddy, will you help me pick out a Christmas tree? Will ya, huh, will ya?

Dad: Well . . . (**Willie** *enters with a snow* [styrofoam] *ball, tosses it at* **Sally**; *she ducks; it hits* **Dad**, *knocking him down behind stage.*)

Sally: Nice shot, arrowhead. You beaned your dad with a slush ball. (**Willie** *hurries to help* **Dad**.)

Willie: Sorry, Dad. You OK?

Dad (*Dryly*): Ever fall backward onto a Christmas tree stand? (*Holds one up that has large nail sticking through it.*)

Willie (*Embarrassed*): Where'd the nail stick?

Dad: The same place it sticks the tree. Now I'm going back by the fire while you kids choose a tree. And don't take all night, either. (*Exits.*)

Sally: Whew. You sure made Dad mad.

Willie: He'll get over it. Now, where were we?

Sally: Hey, look! There's a chipmunk under that tree over there! (*Points at audience.*)

Willie: That's no chipmunk. That's a sprinkler head, dummy.

Sally: Oh . . . Are you sure?

Willie: How many chipmunks do you know that have a garden hose attached?

Sally (*Mocks him*): How many chipmunks do you know that have a garden hose attached? You got a smart mouth, Willie.

Willie: Aw, let's stop arguing and find a Christmas tree. And let's find a big one too, because I'm expecting a record number of presents this year.

Sally: You're probably right—a record low! (*She laughs.*)

Willie (*Sees tree*): How about that one there, Sally? I'll bet all my presents could fit under that one!

Sally: Or on the top of it . . .

Willie: No kiddin' . . . I like this tree! Let's see how much it is. (*Grabs for price tag, knocks tree into* **Sally**, *they fall behind stage.* **Willie** *is looking at* **Sally** *and tree when* **Dad** *enters.*)

Dad (*Doesn't notice accident*): Willie . . . (*He jumps.*)

Willie (*Momentarily shocked*): Oh, Dad! You scared me!

Dad: Sorry. How's the tree hunt going? Did you find a good one yet?

Willie: Uh . . . Oh, sure. Sally's checking it out right now. She and that tree hit it off real good together, as a matter of fact.

Dad: Well, where are they?

Willie: They're talking it over . . .

Dad: Sally is talking to a Christmas tree?

Willie (*Flustered*): Yes. I mean no. I mean . . . Sally's really been swept off her feet, in a manner of speaking, by that tree . . . (**Dad** *scratches head.*)

Sally (*Enters with pine needles sticking out of her hair, and other places*): Ooooh . . . I just got stabbed by eight million pine needles . . .

Dad: Sally! What happened to you? Are you all right?

Willie: A tree fell on her.

Sally: Willie pushed it on me!

Willie: I did not! I was only trying to see the price tag on it!

Dad: OK, OK! You are obviously not hurt, Sally, so let's not make a scene. I'm tired, I'm freezing, and I was bitten by a chipmunk over at the fire. So I'm not in the mood for this.

Sally: See! I told you I saw a chipmunk!

Willie: Are you sure it wasn't a sprinkler?

Dad: Willie, I'm old enough to tell the difference. Now what tree did you kids decide on?

S & W: That one!

Dad: But that one's all beat up and some of the limbs are broken.

Willie: We don't care, Dad. That tree is nice and big.

Sally: Yeah! And besides, me and that tree have been

through a lot together here tonight.

Dad: OK, OK! Go tell the man to come and get it and take it to the flocking room. What color do you want it?

Sally: Pink!

Willie: Purple! (**Sally** *makes a fist.*) Pink!

Dad: OK. Pink it is. Now go tell the man. (*They exit.* **Dad** *speaks to himself.*) I don't know whatever happened to the good ol' simple Christmas we used to have . . . A simple tree, simple decorations, Christmas dinners. Today everything is so complicated and rushed and hectic. It seems like there's no time at all to really enjoy the Christmas spirit and holidays.

Sally (*Enters*): The man said he doesn't have anymore pink and would you mind red?

Dad: RED?

Sally: Thanks, Dad! (*Exits.*)

Dad: A red Christmas tree . . . Oh, well . . . I guess I'll just try to make the most of it. As long as the kids are happy, I'm happy.

Willie (*Enters.*): The man busted off the top of the tree putting it in the truck but he said he'd give you a dollar off, OK, Dad?

Dad: Sure, Willie. (**Willie** *exits, then returns.*)

Willie: The man also said the tree stand would be a dollar extra.

Dad: OK, OK. (**Willie** *exits.*) I guess it's like this for everybody nowadays. But I suppose we'll all find our own little niche of Christmas happiness in the middle of it all . . . We'll find some joy in the giving, in the remembering.

Sally (*Enters*): Dad! Com'ere quick! That chipmunk saw our red Christmas tree and went berserk! He's eating the whole interior of the car! (*Exits.*)

Dad (*Calls after her*): I'm coming, dear, I'm coming. (*To audience.*) On the other hand, I wouldn't trade anything for the crazy wonderful experiences this family's had at Christmas time! Happy Birthday, Merry Christmas! (*Exits.*)

A Christmas Card from the Puppets

by Tom deGraaf

Narrator: During this past year, you have given your wonderful friendship to our puppets. Now, in a token of their appreciation of you, they would like to present a "Christmas Card to you!"

(*Puppets enter singing "Deck the Halls."*)

Dad: Thank you, everybody! Thank you! Because you all have been so nice to us this past year, the kids and I wanted to do a little something special for you at Christmas time. We want to share with you some songs and poems that we hope will make your Christmas celebration just a little bit happier this year. And to start off our program, here is my daughter Sally singing "White Christmas."

(**Sally** *enters alone, sings sweetly with only a few "clinkers." As she starts,* **Willie** *and* **Cool Charlie** *peek out from sides of stage and laugh. Then they start throwing "snow" at* **Sally** *while she sings. They get carried away and the snow really starts flying at her from both sides. On last line "and may all your Christmases be white," they give her a handful of snow right in mouth. She chases them offstage.*)

Dad (*Enters flustered*): Well, uh, that was Sally singing "White Christmas!" And now, my son Willie and Cool Charlie have a Christmas poem for you! (*Applause.*)

Cool (*Reading from notes*): "C" is for Christmas, my favorite time of year, 'cause Dad really panics when his "charge cards" disappear.

Willie (*Reading from notes*): "H" is for the houses, all covered up with snow, each expecting Santa Claus to catch his death of cold.

Cool: "R" is for the relatives who show up at your door. They eat your fudge and watch the game and track the kitchen floor.

Willie: "I" is for my idiot cousin who comes and stays a week. He breaks my toys, makes funny noises, and bites me in my sleep.

Cool: "S" is for the season, winter which it is, a time to snuggle up to girlfriends, yours, not mine or his!

Willie: "T" is for the Christmas tree your doggie dearly loves; he sniffs the limbs and licks the lights, and knocks off half the balls.

Cool: "M" is for Mom, who overspends on gifts because she loves. She buys and buys while Dad is having fits!

Willie: "A" is for the afterglow of that beautiful Christmas morning, when all the love and gifts are shared and Dad is busy snoring.

Cool: "S" of Christmas stands for this lovely row of icicles; they . . .

Willie: Hey, wait a minute! "S" don't stand for "icicles!"

Cool: Ssss! Ssss! Can't you hear that Sssss, dummy? Issssssicles!

Willie: No, you're wrong, Cool Charlie! Icicle starts with "I," not "S."

Cool: Says who? You wanna make something of it? (*He grabs* **Willie**; *they exit arguing.*)

Dad (*Embarrased*): Uh . . . Thank you, Willie and Cool Charlie, for that wonderful Christmas poem. (*Stage shakes as sounds of fight are heard.*) Yes, well, the last part of our Christmas wish to you is a message to you moms and dads out there. And I'd like to give it myself, if you don't mind. (*Pauses, to get serious.*) Christmas can be the most beautiful family experience of the year. It can be a time when families draw closer together in . . .

Sally (*Enters, interrupts*): Dad! Willie and Cool Charlie just flocked my goldfish! I think he's in cardiac arrest!

Come and save 'im, quick!

Willie (*Enters*): Dad! Sally just put my my Christmas gift under the tree and it's leaking sand! I think she gave me another box of sand just like last year! Give her a wappin', Dad!

Cool (*Enters*): Uh, Mr. Weekers! Your wife just came home from shopping and missed the garage door again. You'd better come get the car off the back porch . . . (*All are pressed around* **Dad**, *yelling at same time.*)

Dad (*Slowly puts one hand up to his mouth, tiredly shouts above the noise*): HAVE A MERRY, MERRY CHRISTMAS! (*All exit slowly, yelling.*)

Reprinted from *California Puppets*, Mill Valley, California.
© Copyright 1975. Used by permission.

The Greatest of All Christmas Gifts

by Jim Stewart

Scene I

(**Wally** *enters, Singing "Santa Claus Is Coming to Town."*)

Sarah: Oh, Wally, you're wearing that song out before Christmas ever gets here.

Frankie: Yeah, Wally, can't you sing something else? You're making us all tired of Santa Claus already.

Wally: Well, I happen to really like Christmas, if you guys don't mind!

Maggie: But, Wally, we *all* enjoy Christmas. You just might get too much of a good thing.

Wally: Not when it comes to gettin' presents, I won't! (*Sings, "He's makin' a list, checking it twice, gonna find out who's naughty and nice . . ."*)

Frankie: Boy, Wally, you're just eaten up with presents!

Wally: Yeah, but what a way to go! Surfboards, electric train sets, basketball, sweaters, money, candy. Wowee, I can hardly wait!

Sarah: Wally, you must think that's all there is to Christmas.

Maggie: For sure! it's one thing to enjoy Christmas gifts, but Wally makes a religion out of presents!

Frankie: I've never met a Christmas turkey like you before, Wally.

Sarah: Yeah, man, you beat all I've ever seen. To listen to you talk, the whole purpose for Christmas is to please good ol' Wally!

Wally: What a super thought. I could really clean up, if that were true.

Frankie: You've got a one-track mind, Wally. You know what your attitude makes me want to do to you! Well, I want to rearrange your face! But I won't do it with girls

around. Besides, it probably still wouldn't change your rotten attitude.

Wally: Man, why are you guys gettin's all over my case? Can I help it if I happen to like gifts?

Sarah: There's nothing wrong with liking gifts. All of us like them. But, Wally, you can't talk about anything except your new skateboard, bicycle, and all that other stuff you're so sure you're gonna get!

Maggie: Yeah! I bet you don't know a thing about the joy of giving gifts!

Wally: Sure I do. My folks all tell me how much joy it brings them to give me things. And I enjoy receiving them. That's a great combination!

Maggie, Sarah, Frankie (*Together*): Oh, Wally, come on!

Wally: Cheer up, gang! If you're lucky, I'll let you guys use my new skateboard, every once in a while.

Frankie: Whoopee! How very kind of you. I didn't know turkeys could skate!

Sarah: Yeah, gee thanks, Mr. "Do-Gooder!"

Maggie: Wally, I hope somebody can get the real meaning of Christmas across to you one of these days!

Sarah: It sounds hopeless to me.

Frankie: Yeah, I bet Wally doesn't even know why we really observe Christmas, to begin with.

Wally: Sure I do! Santa Claus invented it many years ago. And, boy, am I glad he did.

Maggie: That does it. Let's leave our "Wally" to "wallow" in his greed. Come on, gang.

Frankie: Yeah, see ya around after you get over your "presentitis!"

Sarah: Don't call us, we'll call you. By the way, Wally, your mother won't need to buy a big turkey for Christmas din-

50

ner. She's already got one! (*All laugh as they exit.*)

Scene II
Christmas Eve

Wally (*Enters alone*): Oh, boy, one more day until Christmas. Sock it to me, all you people who love me so much. I hope everybody remembers I can only open one gift at a time. They're always so thrilled to see me open each package. Christmas is the most funsies I know of. (*Sings.*) "I'm dreaming of a skateboard for Christmas."

Voice (*Offstage*): I think we need to have a talk, Wally.

Wally: Yeah, man, sure. What you wanna . . . (*Looks around.*) Who are you and where are you speaking from?

Voice: This is the voice of God, Wally, and I'm heard in all places, where men are willing to listen to me.

Wally: Come on, man, you're puttin' me on. God doesn't just talk like this to people.

Voice: On the contrary, Wally. I talk with people all the time. However, I must admit you and I haven't talked much lately.

Wally: Hey, God, I'm a good kid. I ate my mom's spinach last night, and baby-sat with my little sister, and . . . and . . . I even plan to share some of my new Christmas gifts occasionally.

Voice: It's your attitude toward Christmas that I'm concerned about, Wally.

Wally: Why? I believe in it. I've even been known to let my grandmother give me a hug as I open her gift.

Voice: Actually, Wally, yours seems to be a rather selfish attitude, in regard to Christmas.

Wally (*Quietly*): Oh, brother, the neighborhood gang and now God himself are after me. This is ridiculous!

Voice: We're not after you, Wally. And it's not ridiculous.

Wally: You weren't supposed to hear what I just said!

Voice: Have you forgotten who I am, Wally?

Wally: Oh? Suffering Skateboards, I forgot that you . . . uh . . . eh . . . that you . . . well . . .

Voice: That I hear everything?

Wally: Yeah, that's it. Uh, Mr. God, sir, what do you mean about my attitude?

Voice: I mean that you ignore the great joy of giving others Christmas gifts. You only know how to receive them, and you don't seem to even remember the greatest gift this world has ever received.

Wally: Gee, you mean there's a skateboard even better than the one I'm gonna get? Wow!

Voice: No, Wally. I gave the greatest gift that's ever been given to you or anyone else, and it was a very, very costly gift for me to give.

Wally: Really, God? How much did it cost?

Voice: It cost me my Son, Wally. My very own Son.

Wally: Holy Halos! You mean Jesus? I never thought of him as a gift before. Why did you have to give your only Son?

Voice: It was the one way I could bring men and women to a proper relationship with myself. Becoming a man was the only way I could be understood in the right way.

Wally: You know, God, I've always wondered why Jesus couldn't have come into this world as a grown man.

Voice: I chose a natural way for him to come into the world—as a little baby—flesh and blood—just like you and everybody else—except that my Son, Jesus, was truly human *and also* truly divine. Man and God were joined together in one person, for the first and only time in history. And my Son was perfect.

Wally: How was Jesus perfect?

Voice: Jesus knew about wrong; he was tempted to do wrong; yet he never did anything wrong. That's perfection.

Wally: Gee, it sure is! Was the world glad when you gave your Son?

Voice: Some people were, Wally. But many people did not understand Jesus. They accused him of being an imposter, a government traitor, a liar, and other terrible things.

Wally: I've always heard about how Jesus went around doing good to others. Why would anyone be against a man like that?

Voice: Because many people's idea of good, Wally, is not necessarily the right kind of good.

Wally: Well, I think I remember the rest of the story.

Voice: Yes, people thought that they could destroy the Son of God by crucifying him on a cross, but they were wrong, Wally—because even though they killed Jesus, he raised up from the grave after three days, to show his victory over death and sin.

Wally: Boy, that was really the work of a magician.

Voice: Not magic, Wally. It was the power of God. Today Jesus lives in heaven and speaks to men through the Holy Spirit.

Wally: You mean when Jesus came back to heaven, he sent someone else to take his place.

Voice: That's right, Wally. Not another physical person, but a Spirit that can live in the heart of every person who believes that Jesus died for his sin. All anyone needs to do is to invite Jesus into his heart—then the Holy Spirit will take up residence in that person's heart.

Wally: Gee! I've heard this story before, but it's never meant this much to me. What does this have to do with Christmas?

Voice: The day you celebrate as Christmas Day, Wally, is the birthday of my Son, Jesus, who was born over two thousand years ago, in a tiny little village called Bethlehem.

Wally: But how do we get presents out of Christmas?

Voice: People give each other gifts in honor of Jesus' birthday—to show their love for each other and for him. Remember that the Wise Men brought gifts to the Baby Jesus on the night he was born.

Wally (*Clears his throat*): Well . . . I . . . er . . . uh . . .

Voice: What are you trying to say, Wally?

Wally: You already know what I'm trying to say, God. You know everything.

Voice: Yes, but it's good for you to be able to say it for your own good.

Wally: OK. Everybody knows that I don't give gifts; I just receive them. But I can change that, God.

Voice: Can you, Wally?

Wally: I certainly can—with your help, that is. In fact, I'm going right now to find some gifts for those I love this Christmas.

Voice: Wally, just remember.

Wally: Remember what?

Voice: It's not the gift itself that means the most. It's what you feel in your heart for people that causes you to want to give.

Wally: I see what you mean now, God. The birthday of Jesus makes Christmas what it is. Gee, who would ever have thought ol' greedy Wally could really be happy about celebrating someone else's birthday?

Voice: That's the spirit, Wally. Our little talk has been worthwhile, I can tell.

Wally (*To audience*): I know what I'm gonna do tomorrow on Christmas day. When all my family, relatives, and friends are gathered together, I'm gonna get out my dusty old Bible and read the story of Jesus' birth to everyone. I bet it'll make this Christmas the best one my family and I have ever had. In fact, I think I'll find some friends and sing my favorite Christmas carol, "Joy to the World." (*Shouts off-stage.*). Hey, Maggie. Sarah, Frankie, and everyone in the audience, C'mon, let's sing! (*Everybody sings "Joy to the World."*)

The Christmas Spirit

by Sam Everett

Scene I

Elmer: Hi, Ralph!

Ralph: Hi, Elmer! Say, what's that? Whatcha got?

Elmer: It's a jar! Yeah—this is my jar. How do ya like it, huh?

Ralph: Well, let's see. It's glass—it's round—it's got a hole at the top—it's got a bottom—it's a jar, all right—a pretty nice jar—yes . . . that's a nice jar. What's it for?

Elmer: I was thinking . . . I could paint it green—green with red stripes. How about that? Whadda ya think? Green with red stripes? How would that be, huh, Ralph?

Ralph: Well, then you'd have a jar—painted green and red. What are you gonna do with it?

Elmer: Or I could paint it red. Yeah! Red with green stripes. That'd be nice. Say, Ralph, which one is best—green with red stripes or red with green stripes? Which one, Ralph?

Ralph: Elmer! What's going on? What are you doing with that jar! Green, red—red, green! How should I know, unless you tell me what the jar's for?

Elmer: Oh. Well, this jar is for the Christmas spirit.

Ralph: The Christmas spirit?

Elmer: Yep, gonna get me some. Put it right here?

Ralph: You're gonna put it in the jar?

Elmer: Yep.

Ralph: The Christmas spirit?

Elmer: Oh, yeah. Everybody always says the Christmas spirit is so great. Well, I'm gonna get some. I'll have some now and then the whole rest of the year. Whenever I want to, I'll just open this jar and take a little out.

Ralph: Elmer!

Elmer: It'll be great. I can't wait.

Ralph: Elmer!

Elmer: Boy, this is gonna be my best year ever!

Ralph: Elmer! Elmer, you can't do that! You can't put the Christmas spirit in a jar!

Elmer: Well, sure, not right now. But when I grab it—then you'll see. I'll just grab it, and zip, right in the ole jar.

Ralph: Elmer, you can't catch the Christmas spirit in your hand anymore than you can catch a butterfly. You can't grab it with your hand.

Elmer: You can't?

Ralph: Nope!

Elmer: Say, thanks, Ralph. Oh. Ralph?

Ralph: Yeah?

Elmer: Could I borrow your hammer?

Ralph: My hammer? What for?

Elmer: I'm gonna build a trap to catch the Christmas spirit.

Ralph: Good grief!

Scene II

(**Betty, Ralph** *enter*)

Betty: It's Elmer!

(**Elmer** *enters, swinging net—may be large tropical fish net.*) Swish! Swish!

Ralph: Elmer!

(**Elmer** *keeps swinging.*) Swish!

Betty: Elmer! What on earth are you doing with that butterfly net?

Elmer: I got it this time. Now listen—you can't get the Christmas spirit in your hand, right?

Betty: Right. Yep, that's right!

Elmer: But I'm gonna scoop it up in this net. It'll come by, and then—zap! I'll catch it in this neat net, then I'll put it in this cage I built!

Ralph: A net! A cage! I don't believe it. You really think it'll work?

Elmer: It's a sure thing. I don know why I didn't think of this before. Now, see, I can have the Christmas spirit all year.

Betty: No, no, no, Elmer! You can't do it that way either! You can't get the Christmas spirit with a net. Now stop that silliness!

Elmer: OK. OK. Now let me see. You can't get the Christmas spirit in a jar; you can't keep it in a cage.

Ralph: Right so far!

Elmer: You can't grab it with your hand! And you can't trap it in a net!

Betty: Right!

Elmer: I guess you can't catch it in a bear trap either.

Ralph: That's right!

Elmer: Or a hole in the ground?

Betty: Nope.

Elmer: Am empty box?

Ralph: Nope.

Elmer: You can't catch it at all, can you?

Betty: Nope!

Elmer: I think I understand now. Thanks, thanks a lot.

Betty: Boy, I was pretty worried, Elmer. I mean—

Elmer (*Whistles, as for a dog*): Here, Christmas Spirit! Here, Christmas—

Ralph (*Interrupts*): Elmer, what are you doing now?

Elmer: Well, if I can't catch it, then I'm gonna let it come to me; then if I'm nice eno gh, maybe it'll come and stay. Got it?

Betty & Ralph: Oh, wow!

Scene III

Elmer: Hey, Ralph, old buddy. I finally got it!

Ralph: You did? That's great, Elmer. You mean you've been thinking about the Christmas spirit, and you've finally got it?

Elmer: Oh, yeah. And it's really pretty simple, isn't it?

Ralph: Why, sure. It really is.

Elmer: So here, you take this bag of presents here.

Ralph: Hey, that's nice; thanks, Elmer.

Elmer: Now give them to me. There's some really good things in there—there's a ball, some cars, a train—a football helmet—lots of stuff you can give me.

Ralph: Now, uh . . .

(**Betty** *enters*.)

Elmer: Why don't you give me the ball? That's nice.

Ralph: Elmer, I, uh . . .

Elmer: Give me the train—it's the big blue present down there on the bottom.

Ralph: Uh, the big blue, uh, no, I . . .

Elmer: That's a car—give me the car, then. Boy, this Christmas spirit is really fun. I can't wait. Give me the top next—Wow! This is the best ever! I wish I had this a long time ago.

Betty: Elmer!

Elmer: What, Betty! Hi!

Betty: Elmer, that's not the Christmas spirit—you're just getting stuff.

Elmer: Wait a minute. The Christmas spirit is all about giving, isn't it?

Betty: Yes.

Elmer: And you're giving, aren't you?

Ralph: Yep.

Elmer: The Christmas spirit is giving, and you're giving, and I'm getting it. Boy, this is just great. Next I can get a swimming pool, and an elephant, and a pony, and—

Ralph: Elmer, that's not the Christmas spirit.

Elmer: No?

Betty: No. You're just being selfish in another way. Having the Christmas spirit means being unselfish—it means giving to people—not getting them to give things to you.

Elmer: Oh. Oh! See you later.

Scene IV

Ralph: Hi, Elmer.

Betty: Hi, Elmer, what's up?

Elmer: I've really got the Christmas spirit now, folks. Here. I want to give you a present.

Ralph: Why, thanks, Elmer.

Elmer: Here's a sock. I lost the other one when I was washing it. It's OK 'cause it has a hole in it. And here's some jelly I don't like—it's tomato jelly and it tastes kinda funny on my toast.

Betty: You numbskull! What are you doing?

Elmer: I'm giving Ralph these presents.

Betty: Those aren't presents. That's stuff you don't want.

Elmer: That's right. Why would I give away good stuff? I don't want to give away real neat things I like.

Ralph: Well that's sure not the Christmas spirit.

Elmer: It's pretty good to me.

Betty: We have the Christmas spirit when we realize that God gives us the very best things he can. It was that first Christmas, you know, when God gave us his Son.

Elmer: He really gives us his best?

Ralph: You bet he does.

Elmer: Wow, he must really love us a lot—to be that kind.

Ralph: I think you're about to get it, Elmer. Now tell me, how do you feel?

Elmer: Feel?

Betty: Yeah, how does it make you feel?

Elmer: Well, I guess . . . God is the greatest there ever has been.

Ralph: Yep.

Elmer: And he loves us all . . .

Betty: Yep.

Elmer: Loves us enough to give us Jesus, his Son . . . on Christmas.

Ralph: Yep . . . Yep . . .

Elmer: So . . . that . . . makes . . . me . . . want . . . to . . . be . . . kind . . . to others. Yeah! That's it! I really want to do something nice for other people.

Betty & Ralph: You got it, Elmer!

Elmer: I got it?

Betty & Ralph: The Christmas Spirit! You got it!

Elmer: Naw—can't be—it's too simple! See ya later.

Puppy Love

by Marianne Hawkins

(*Two dog puppets enter.*)

Sam: Oh, Sandy, you should see the good-looking poodle that just moved in down the street!

Sandy: Yeah? What's so unusual about her?

Sam (*Eagerly*): Well, she barks with the cutest French accent and wears all kinds of fancy sweaters and ribbons in her hair and stuff like that!

Sandy (*Mischievously*): Uh-oh! sounds like you've got it bad!

Sam (*Moaning*): Oh . . . I tell you what, Sandy, I think I'm in *love*!

Sandy (*Giggles*): What do you know about love? You've just got a bad case of *puppy love*!

Sam (*Emphatically*): Well, this puppy knows real love when he sees it. (*Pause.*) Hey—I think I'll send her a valentine. How's this?

> Roses are red,
> Violets are blue,
> Hey, poodle,
> This hounddog's
> in love with you!

Sandy (*Groans, coughs, etc.*): Uh, well, uh, that's *original*, anyway, Sam!

Sam (*Miserable*): Oh, she doesn't even know I exist. I've just got to think of some way to get to meet her. This is *it*, Sandy . . . the real thing . . . true love. (*Moans.*)

Sandy: Well, hang in there, pal. Sooner or later that poodle is sure to notice what a charming, handsome hound you are.

Sam (*Mournfully*): Yeah, I guess you're right! But until she does, life is going to be miserable! I'm going to go write her a love letter. See you later. (*Exits while saying next line.*) Let's see now, Roses are red . . .

Sandy: Poor ol' Sam. I guess it is the time of year when lots of folks are thinking about love. But you know, there's one kind of love that is stronger and deeper than any other kind of love. Sam feels a bad case of puppy love right now, but I am talking about a love that transcends all others—God's love for every one of us!

God loves us so much that he was willing to let Jesus, his only Son, die on the cross to pay for all the sins of the world.

You can experience this real love in your life if you let Jesus live in your heart. Why don't you ask him to forgive you of all your sins and be the Lord and Savior of your life? He promised to do this if we will just let Him. (*Sandy exits.*)

Play for Puppets Who Forgot to Practice

by E. Kay Clark

Fred (*Enters honking horn*): Happy New Year! It's almost here! I'm ready to help with a New Year's show! Happy New Year!

Freida (*Enters*): Hey! Well, here I am, Freddie. Goodness, I didn't want to come. I was watching the _____ game and ____ was ahead. Why are we here, anyway? We haven't practiced anything.

Fred: Our pastor asked us to come. We can do it. There's still time to practice.

Father Time (*Enters*): Time, time . . . did someone call my name? Tonight's my night to do my thing. All year long folks mention my name, but nowhere like now, the last night of the year. I get letters that say things like:

"I wish I had taken more time to be nice"; "If I had more time, I would help someone"; "I need more time to help with homework"; "I would have passed that test if I had more time."

Well, ha ha to everyone—regrets are well meant, but I'm in control tonight. There's no more this year after a little bit.

> Goodbye to this very old year
> Farewell to those memories dear
> No more politics, fairs, and conventions
> And forget all those good intentions
> The year 198_ is soon in the past
> Only the time in the future will last.
> Time waits for no one—not even you
> So if there's something that you meant to do
> Forget it . . . The year is through.

Ha Ha Ha . . . Hee hee hee . . . Another year dies . . .

Time does flee! (*Exits.*)

Fred: My, he's strange.

Frieda: He's not exactly nice, either.

Fred: I don't think he means to be ugly, he's just always in a hurry.

Frieda: You know, I wish we had taken time to practice . . .

Tru and Ruth (*Enter*): Hi, gang! We are glad you are here. We think church is a nice place to be on New Year's Eve.

Frieda (*Whispering*): Not unless there's a TV set so we can watch the _____ game.

Fred: Sssshshshshshshhhhhhh!

Ruth: Frieda, you were looking a little sad when we arrived. What's up?

Frieda: I've got a case of the "wish-I-hads," and "maybe I should have dones." The end of the year is depressing.

Tru: Not always. I'm looking forward to the new year. It's a chance to catch "maybe I can" and "I think-I-will-itus."

Ruth: Yes, that's why New Year's resolutions are so popular.

Fred (*Loudly*): I resolve . . . .

> To learn to use a skateboard better
> To eat less
> To sleep more
> And not to leave my room a mess.

Tru: That's OK, Fred, but where does God's will fit into all this?

Ruth: Right—remember that God is in control of time. There's no need to feel badly about what was left undone in this past year. What's important is to ask forgiveness and try to do better in the New Year.

Frieda: Wow . . . you mean another chance, a whole new year to try again! I like that idea. It makes me really excited about what might happen.

Fred: Yep. I think so too. What you are talking about is hope. I hope I'm happy in the New Year. I hope I get lots of money. I hope we practice before we do another people show. I hope I get a three-wheel bike I didn't get this Christmas.

Frieda: I hope all the old maids get married so they quit chasing _____ (single bachelor in church).

Tru: Wait a minute: Hope is OK, but that's not enough. You must have foam rubber for brains! (*Puppets look at each other, then nod.*) You need to trust God to take care of you. If Jesus is your Savior, he will control your life if you let him.

Fred: You are talking to them out there, our people friends. Puppets can't accept Christ, but people can. All you football fans . . . Listen to what Tru and Ruth say. They have the answer to a really Happy New Year.

Frieda: Freddie, let's try to do our show, even though we might make mistakes. They won't care. Let's do it together. Ready?

Father Time (*Enters*): Hold it. I want to be part of the program too.

All puppets together: We are sad to see the old year go

> But a better one's coming along and so . . .
> Put off your sadness, gloom and regret,
> God's chosen people have no reason to fret.
> Do away with complaining and making excuses,
> A person who gripes is the one who loses;
> Smile, pray, and play and sing,
> Read your Bible and praise the King.
> The God of forgiveness is still on his throne,
> You don't have to start a New Year alone.
> So off with the old year, on with the new;
> We wish you God's blessings,
> Happy New Year to you.

(*Puppets bow, exit.*)

America, My Country

by Marianne Hawkins

(Susie, Johnnie, *and* Freddie *enter.* Susie *carries a small American flag.*)

Susie: I just love the Fourth of July!

Johnnie (*Eagerly agrees*): Me, too! I like the parades and the picnics!

Freddie: I like the fireworks!

Susie: You know, fellas, I am glad that I live in the United States. Our country has some problems, but it is still the best place of all!

Freddie: You're right, Susie. America is my country and I'm proud of it!

Johnnie: Me, too, Freddie! I guess the most important thing about the Fourth of July is that it makes people stop and think about how much they love America.

Susie: I love America because I am free to choose where I live.

Freddie: I love America because I can be what I want to be!

Johnnie: You're both right! Our country gives us the right to make our own choices. In some places, the government tells people exactly what to do. They force them to work at a certain place, live a certain way—but not in America! We are free to choose!

Freddie: I love America because *all* people are free—not just a chosen few!

Susie: I love America because we can talk about our problems and work together to solve them!

Johnnie: I love America because we are free to read the Bible, pray, go to church, and worship God as we want to.

Freddie: Did you know that in some places people are put in jail if they are caught reading the Bible or praying?

Susie (*Shocked*): Really! I didn't know that. Wow, I think we should really be thankful for our country. Imagine what it would be like if we couldn't go to church or talk about God.

Johnnie: God has blessed our country with lots of riches. We have more natural resources and a better way of life than any other place in the world. It's time that Americans began to realize this.

Freddie: You're right, John. People all across America should thank God for giving us a great country like the United States.

Susie: We should also pray for our president and other government leaders. God can give them the wisdom it will take to make our country even greater!

Johnnie: You're right, Susie. If Americans really depended on God, a lot of our problems could be solved!

Freddie: I guess it is up to people like us to begin to change our country. Christians should be good citizens!

Susie: I never thought about that, Freddie. But it is our responsibility, isn't it?

Johnnie: It sure is! America is our country—it's up to us to make it better.

Freddie: Look! The fireworks are starting! Let's go over on the hill to watch them!

Susie: Yeah! We can see good from there!

(*They begin to exit.* **Johnnie** *remains behind.*)

Susie: Come on, Johnnie!

Johnnie: I'll be there in a minute, Susie!

(*After they exit,* **Johnnie** *bows head and prays.*) God, thank you for my country. I am really proud to say that I am an American. Help our president and the people who work with him to make the right decisions for our country. God, help people all across our nation to depend on you. You have given us a beautiful place to live. Help us to take care of it and keep it a place of freedom. Thank you, God, for letting me be an American. Amen. (**Johnnie** *exits.*) Wow! Just look at those fireworks!

Oh, Yes, Thank You

by Danny E. Bush

(*Props: 2 rakes, a basket, some leaves, 2 trees, two cups or small jugs*)

Milton: Hey, Mark, hand me the rake!

Mark: OK, OK.

Milton: We've got to get these leaves up before it snows.

Mark: Yeah, before it snows.

Milton (*Rakes*): Minnie wants everything cleaned up for Thanksgiving.

Mark (*Carries a basket of leaves*): Yeah, for Thanksgiving.

Milton: Thanksgiving, Thanksgiving. That's all Minnie, my dear sister, has talked about for a month.

Mark: Yeah, for a month. For a month? That sure is a long time to think about Thanksgiving.

Milton: Minnie says we should be thankful all year round.

Mark: Yeah, all year round. Right now I'd be thankful to get all this yardwork done.

Milton: Me too, Mark.

Minnie: Hi, Milton and Mark!

Milton and Mark: Hi, Minnie!

Minnie: I brought you some lemonade and wanted to tell you both how . . .

Milton: Great, I'm thirsty! (*Grabs a cup from* **Minnie**.)

Mark: Yeah, me too! (*Grabs a cup from* **Minnie**.)

Milton (*Loud drinking sound*): Glug, glug.

Mark((*Loud drinking sound*): Yeah, glug, glug.

Minnie: Milton and Mark! You could at least say thank you before you start glugging!

Milton: Oh, yes, thank you!

Mark: Oh, yes, thank you!

Minnie: "Oh, yes, thank you." You know, you two are getting like a lot of people. "Thank you" to many people is just something nice to say but they don't mean it.

Milton: I feel a Thanksgiving sermon coming.

Mark: Yeah, a Thanksgiving sermon.

Minnie: Well, you two guys need to learn more about being really thankful.

Milton: How about you, Minnie?

Mark: Yeah, how about you, Minnie? Hey, Milton, what about her?

Milton: Minnie keeps talking about being thankful. Here we are raking leaves and I haven't heard her say thank you.

Mark: Yeah, she hasn't said thank you.

Minnie: Just what do you think this lemonade is?

Milton: It's good!

Mark: Yeah, it's good!

Minnie: Bringing you the lemonade is a way of saying "thank you." Besides, I was about to say thank you when you two grabbed the lemonade and started glugging!

Milton: Minnie, we're sorry.

Mark: Yeah, we're sorry. Hey, Milton, what are we sorry for?

Milton: We're sorry we didn't say thank you and mean it, Minnie.

Mark: Oh, yeah, well we really mean thank you, Minnie.

Milton: Very good, Mark.

Matt (*Enters singing*): "Come, ye thankful people, come. Raise the song of harvest home! mmmm, mmmmmm, mmmmmm." Hello, everybody. What's happening?

Milton: We just learned to say thank you.

Matt: Thank you? That seems simple enough.

Mark: Not the way Minnie wants us to say thank you.

Matt: What do you mean?

Milton: Minnie reminded us that when we say thank you we should really mean it.

Matt: I see what you mean.

Minnie: God is good to us all year round. Thanksgiving is a special time to tell God thank you and mean it.

Mark: I really mean it, Minnie. Now, can we finish raking the leaves before it gets dark?

Matt: Hand me a rake and I'll help.

Milton (*Handing* **Matt** *a rake*): Here you go, Matt, and thank you.

Mark: Yeah, thank you, Matt, and we really mean it!

Minnie: There may be hope for you guys yet!

> (**Matt** hums "*Come, Ye Thankful People, Come.*"
> **Minnie, Milton,** and **Mark** *join in humming.*)

Milton: You know, it feels good to thank one another and God.

Mark: Yeah, it feels good to be thankful.

Minnie, Milton, Mark, and **Matt** (*Together*): OH, YES, THANK YOU!

Leader (*Optional*): From the Psalms comes this verse: "O give thanks to the Lord, for he is good; for his steadfast love endures for ever!" (Ps. 118:29) Milton, Mark, Matt, and Minnie remind you and me that God is good and that we can be very thankful for his goodness and love throughout the year.

Thanksgiving

by Marianne Hawkins

(*Puppets enter together, talking.*)

Susie: Johnnie, what do you think about when you hear the word Thanksgiving?

Johnnie (*Excitedly*): Turkey!

Susie: Oh, Johnnie. What else!

Johnnie: Pumpkin pie, potatoes, gravy, turkey and dressing, and cakes and . . .

Susie: But Johnnie, there's more to Thanksgiving than food!

Johnnie: Yeah! We get a holiday from school. No homework for five days . . . oh boy!

Susie: Johnnie, there are still more important things than that.

Johnnie: What could be more important than being out of school?

Susie (*Disgusted*): Johnnie, don't you understand anything?

Johnnie (*Giggles*): Sure, Susie, I was just teasing you! Thanksgiving is a special day. We should take time to realize all of the blessings God has given us!

Susie: Like our family and friends . . .

Johnnie: Our homes and churches . . . even our schools! God gives us everything we need.

Susie: We should be grateful and thankful for God's blessings! Psalm 100:4 says, "Enter into his gates with Thanksgiving, and into his courts with praise: be thankful unto him, and bless his name."

Johnnie: That just means to thank God for everything he has done for us!

Susie: That's a good way to show God that we love him.

Johnnie: Susie, what are some of the things that you are thankful for?

Susie: I have lots of things—my mom, my dad, and all my family, my house, my teachers, and my friends like you!

Johnnie: I'm thankful for those things too, Susie!

Susie: But you know, Johnnie, most of all I'm thankful that Jesus loves me and lives in my heart.

Johnnie: That's the best thing I know of to be thankful for, Susie.

Susie: Johnnie, let's pray together and thank God for all of our blessings!

Johnnie: OK, Susie. (*To audience.*) Would you bow your heads and close your eyes and pray with us? (*Pause.*) Dear God, thank you very much for all of our friends who come to church here. Thank you for our buses and our bus workers. Thank you for our pastor and other teachers who help us to learn about you . . .

Susie: And God, thank you for Jesus, who lives in our hearts. Thank you for loving us. We love you, God, and thank you for everything you do for us. Amen.

Johnnie: Amen! (*To* **Susie.**) You know, we could never thank God for everything he does for us. It sure makes you feel good inside when you know God loves you.

Susie: I know what you mean, Johnnie. Well, I hope all of our friends have a nice Thanksgiving and remember to thank God for all their blessings!

Johnnie: I'm sure they will! (*To audience.*) See you later! (*They exit.*)

Section IV

GENERAL

All Aboard for Heaven!

by Marianne Hawkins

(*Props: Poster of train covering front of puppet stage to simulate the Gospel Express. One puppet should be dressed as a conductor.*)

Conductor (*Stands beside train and calls loudly*): All aboard! Last call for heaven! All aboard!

Puppet 1 (*Rushes up to* **Conductor** *and hands him a ticket*): I thought I was late! I was out taking food to the poor and needy!

Conductor: This ticket says "Good Works." You can't go to heaven by good works! The Bible says that we are saved *for* good works, not by them!

Puppet 1 (*Frantically*): What do you mean? I can't go to heaven? But I have been a Sunday School teacher, a member of the building committee, an usher, a deacon; I've taken food and clothes to the needy .... none of this will get me to heaven? (*Exits sobbing.*)

(**Conductor** *shakes head sadly and then turns to greet* **Puppet 2.**)

Puppet 2 (*Enters singing anthems*): Good morning, Conductor. I'm ready to go to heaven. I am sure they can use me in the heavenly choir!

Conductor (*Looks down at ticket*): This ticket says "Choir Member." That won't take you to heaven!

Puppet 2: There must be some mistake. You see, I have the best voice in the whole choir. I have sung many solos and performed in many important places.

Conductor (*Shakes head*): I'm sorry. That's not the right ticket.

(**Puppet 2** *exits very dejected.*)

Puppet 3 (*Dressed very extravagantly*): Here I am, Conductor. I do hope you have a good compartment vacant. After all, I am a very rich person and an important church member.

Conductor: Your ticket says "Tithes and Offerings." That won't take you to heaven!

Puppet 3 (*Leaves angrily while saying his line*): After all that money I sacrificed? Of all the nerve—I'll buy my way to heaven yet! You just wait and see!

Conductor (*Calls loudly*): All aboard! Last call for heaven!

Puppet 4 (*Enters and speaks to conductor in a very knowledgeable tone of voice*): I have arrived, kind sir. Would you please direct me to a seat with good lighting? I must read and study as we travel.

Conductor: Wait a minute—your ticket says "Wisdom and Knowledge."

Puppet 4: That is correct, sir. I have devoted my life to a study of the Scriptures. I have a great knowledge of religious history.

Conductor: I am afraid that won't take you to heaven, sir.

Puppet 4 (*Haughtily*): Whatever do you mean? I am much more intelligent than you could ever hope to be. (*Exits angrily.*)

Conductor (*Sighs*): Isn't there *anyone* to ride the train?

Puppet 5 (*Enters shyly*): Sir, I'd like to ride the train.

Conductor: Where is your ticket?

Puppet 5: Ticket? I don't have a ticket.

Conductor: You can't ride the train without the right ticket.

Puppet 5 (*Meekly*): But sir, I don't have a fancy ticket. All I have to offer you is Jesus! He lives in my heart!

Conductor (*Kindly*): That's all you need, my friend. Welcome aboard the train! (**Puppet 5** *boards the train and waits as* **Conductor** *speaks to audience.*) Are you ready to get on board the train? What does your ticket say? Perhaps you had better make sure that it says "Jesus." Jesus said, "I am the way, the truth, and the life. No man comes to the father but through me." What does your ticket say, friends? (*Calls loudly.*) All aboard, last call for heaven!

(*A spotlight would be effective in this skit so that it could be ended by an abrupt moment of darkness.*)

Wages of Sin

by Debbie Smith

(Props: 3 signs—"The Wages," "of Sin is," "Death"—gift box, paper money.)

(Puppets turn over sign, "The Wages.")
#1 *(Whistling, sees words, stops)*: Hum. I wonder what this is. *(Reads.)* The Wages. Hum. The Wages. I wonder what that means.
#2: Hi, Joe. I've been looking all over for you.
#1: Well, here I am.
#2: I owe you these wages.
#1: Wages, huh?
#2: Yes, you did some work for me last week and I need to pay you for it.
#1: So what you pay me is my wages?
#2: Yes, I owe it to you. I must pay you your wage. Here. *(Gives it to him.)* Goodbye.
#1: Thanks, see you later.
   (Puppets turn over next sign, "of Sin is.")
#1: I wonder what it says now. "The wages of sin is." Hot dog! You mean I'm gonna get paid for sinning. That's not bad. Nothing like getting paid for something I enjoy doing.
   (Puppets turn over last sign, "Death.")
#1: Death! The wages of sin is *death!* Oh, no, I'm gonna die. I don't want to die. Oh, no! I'm too young to die!

#3: Joe, what's the matter?
#1: I'm gonna die!
#3: How do you know?
#1: Because the wages of sin is death!
#3: Joe, I have a gift for you that I want you to have. *(Gives him gift.)*
#1: Why would I want a gift when I'm about to die? The way I've been sinning, it could be any minute.
#3: Just open it.
*(Opens box)*: It has a message in it.
#3: Read the message.
#1: It says "The wages of sin is death." I already knew that!
#3: Finish it.
#1 *(reading)*: "But the free gift is eternal life through Jesus Christ our Lord."
#3: Isn't that great, Joe?
#1: Eternal life is free?
#3: Jesus paid the debt we owed for our sin when he died on the cross.
#1: Jesus paid for my sinning?
#3: Yes, Jesus paid the full price. You just accept the free gift of his Son, and you have eternal life.

A Saved Sinner

by Greg George

#1 *(To himself)*: Why did I do that? Why? Why? Why? Why did I do it?
#2 *(Enters)*: Why did you do what?
#1: Sin! That's what.
#2: What do you mean, why did you sin?
#1: How much clearer can I get? *(Louder and right in the face of #2.)* Why-did-I-sin?
#2: Oh!—Why did you sin? Well, that's a dumb question to ask.
#1: Dumb! Did you say dumb?
#2: Yes, I said dumb. D - U - M - B.
#1: And just why is it dumb to ask, "Why did I sin?"
#2: Because the Bible says in Romans 3:23, "All have sinned."
#1 *(Quickly)*: All have sinned! You mean everybody?
#2: That's right, everybody except Jesus has sinned.
#1 *(Surprised)*: Even you?

#2: I'm afraid even I have sinned.
#1 *(Sharply)*: Ohhh! That makes you a sinner like me.
#2: You're right, I'm a sinner; but I'm a saved sinner.
#1: A saved sinner! What's a saved sinner?
#2: A saved sinner is a person who has repented of his sins and confessed them before God and has asked Jesus to save him.
#1: I don't understand!
#2: It's like this: If a person stays a sinner, the Bible says in Romans 6:23, "The wages of sin is death."
#1 *(Quickly)*: Death!
#2: That's right, death and separation from God for eternity.
#1: Forever, and ever, and ever?
#2: Uh huh, but that's not what God wants.
#1: What does God want?
#2: God wants everybody to be saved, but he gives us a

free choice.

#1: He does?

#2: Yeah, Romans 5:8 says, "God commended (or showed) his love for us, in that, while we were yet sinners, Christ died for us."

#1: You mean Jesus died for me, even though I'm a sinner?

#2: Yes sir, he even died for you, a sinner. But you can become a saved sinner like me if you want to.

#1: I can?

#2: Of course. The Bible says in Romans 10:13, "For everyone who calls upon the name of the Lord will be saved."

#1: Man, that's great, but come on quick.

#2: Where to?

#1: To tell my brother so he can be saved like I'm going to be. (*They exit.*)

Is Jesus Inside of You?

by Ann Brandon

Herman: Hi, boys and girls! I brought a friend with me today. His name is Dog. Dog, where are you?

Dog: Hi, Herman! (*A person walks across in front of puppets.*) What was that?

Herman: What? I didn't see anything. (*Person walks back across.*)

Dog: There it goes again.

Herman: Oh, that. That's just a person.

Dog: A person? What's a person?

Herman: People are very funny creatures. None of them is alike. Each one of them is very different, and you can never tell what they'll do or say. They can do anything. Why, sometimes they do something just because that's the way they've always done it and they do the same thing, the same way, over and over again. Some of them won't do some things just because they're done a new or different way . . . and then there are some that are always trying to be different and do different things.

Dog: Herman, you were right. They sure are funny.

Herman: That's not all! You haven't heard anything yet. You know how we always say just what we are supposed to say? Well, they say whatever they want . . . and sometimes they don't even mean what they say.

Dog: You mean they say one thing and do another?

Herman: That's right. But they're not all bad. Some of them really try to do their best. Besides, without them, we would be empty inside; and life just wouldn't be the same without them. You know what I mean. (*Looks at the curtain.*) People are the ones that make us what we are.

Dog: Now I understand. We're empty and not complete without people; but people are just like us because they are empty and incomplete without Jesus inside of them.

Boeing's Concept of God

by Jackie Kemp

(*Dialogue takes place between a caterpillar marionette and* **Puppeteer**)

Puppeteer: Well, Boeing, we have to leave now. Is there anything you'd like to say before we leave this nice audience?

Boeing: There is just one little question I'd like to ask.

Puppeteer: It had better be brief since we're almost out of time.

Boeing: Are you God?

Puppeteer: Huh? Am I God?

Boeing: That's my question: Are you God?

Puppeteer: Ah—no! But where in the world did you ever get an idea like that?

Boeing: Well, you're *always* up there, and I'm *always* down here!

Puppeteer: Boeing, if you've really noticed, I'm not that much further above you. Actually, there are probably plenty of people here who are taller than I.

Boeing: I guess you're right.

Puppeteer: Is that your only reason, since that isn't such a good one?

Boeing: Well-l-l, God runs the show and organizes things; and when it comes to puppet shows, you do that.

Puppeteer: You're right about that. God does run the show; but, Boeing, I only run things when it comes to puppet shows. And the only time I'm organized is during a show. Now then, you certainly must have a much better reason than that!

Boeing: One thing I know for sure about God is that he is the Creator. Who created me?

Puppeteer: I did . . . but that doesn't make me God. Boeing, you see all those people out there? Well, God created all of them! I can only create puppets made of felt, foam, fur, and fabric. But God can create even more than that. All of these people here are filled with ideas and have talents and skills. God created all that they can do. God created

creativity. You see?

Boeing: Yes, I guess so.

Puppeteer: There is one more fact about God that really will help you understand even more about God. God really loves and cares for us. You know that I love you. Do you remember a few weeks ago when one of your foot strings broke and I repaired it? I did that because I cared for you. But God cares for all of us even more than I care for you. God loved us and cared for us so much that he sent his Son to die for us. Boeing, I love you; but I really doubt that I love you enough to be willing to die for you. You see, God really loves and cares.

Boeing: Wow! That really is great.

Puppeteer: I hope you understand.

Boeing: I do.

Puppeteer: Even though I'm not what you thought I was, I hope you'll continue to like me. And I'll always take care of you. OK?

Boeing: OK.

Puppeteer: We have to go now; say goodbye.

Jesus Taught About God's Love

by Rick Brown

(**Helen** *is reading Bible.*)

Danny: Hey, Helen! What are you reading?

Helen: I'm reading a parable in the Bible.

Danny (*Scratching head*): I didn't know that there were a pair of bulls in the Bible.

Helen (*Exasperated*): I didn't say "a pair of bulls." I said "parable."

Danny: What's a parable?

Helen: Well, it's a . . . I'm not sure. I've got an idea. Let's look it up in my nifty Bible dictionary. (*Exits, returns with book.*) Parable . . . parable . . . Oh! Here it is. Parable—an earthly message to teach spiritual things.

Danny: What was the parable about that you were reading?

Helen: Oh! It was in Luke, chapter 15, about a sheep that got lost, and a lady who lost a coin, and a boy who ran away from home.

Danny: Well, that's the earthly message, but what does it teach us about spiritual things?

Helen (*Scratching head*): Uh . . . well . . . what do you think?

Danny: I asked you first.

Helen (*Pauses*): It tells about things that were lost—a sheep, a coin, and a son. Wonder what God is trying to tell us?

Danny: Is there a verse in the parable that says something about you?

Helen: Me?

Danny: No! Is there a verse that has the word you in it?

Helen: I don't know. Let me see. (*Scans page.*) Here it is, in verse 7. It says . . . "I say unto you, that likewise joy shall be in heaven over one sinner that repenteth, more than over ninety and nine just persons, which need no repentance."

Danny: So what does that have to do with a lost coin . . . or a lost sheep . . . or a lost son?

Helen: It means that God loves everybody, even you. And he wants every single person to accept Jesus as his personal Lord and Savior. If you don't, then you're "lost."

Danny: Oh! I understand now.

Helen: Now let me get back to reading more parables.

Danny: But I thought you said that there wasn't a pair of bulls in the Bible!

Where's "It" At?

by Jeff Wyers

(*Props: Cardboard TV, stacks of books, cardboard guitar and rock music, play money, antennaes or cardboard spaceship.*)

Betty: Hi, everybody. How are you? I'm glad to see you're here and so happy. It's really great to be happy.

Randy (*Enters*): Hey, Baby! What's happenin'? Where's "It" at?

Betty: Huh? (*Looks at audience, confused.*)

Randy: Somebody told me you really knew where it was. Where's "It" at?

Betty: "It"? What's "It"?

Randy: Aw, haw-haw, don't joke with me! C'mon, share. Where's "It" at?

Betty: Really, what's "It"?

Randy: You know, "It."— (*Fast, run together.*)—Peace love joy smiles warmth meaning happiness satisfaction wealth contentment fullfillment truth goodness pureness and wisdom!

Betty (*To audience*): What'd he say?

Randy: I said: Peace love joy smiles warmth meaning happiness satisfaction wealth contentment fullfillment truth goodness pureness and wisdom! (*Shouts.*) "It"!

Betty: Peace, warmth, happiness . . . Oh! I know what you mean!

Randy: Yes, "It"!—Wait, lemme guess . . .

Betty: I'll give you a clue. "It" means *joy!*

Randy: Ah . . . I know. "It's" . . . "It's" a television. (*Pop up TV.*) Right, huh? "It's" a TV!

Betty: Are you kidding? That might bring smiles once in a while, but meaning? And what about wisdom?

Randy: Oh, well, uh . . . (*Remove TV.*) Wisdom, huh? It's, It's . . . Education! Right? Right! Huh? (*Stack of books appears.*)

Betty: Well, that's got meaning and some wisdom . . . but what about warmth and joy?

Randy: That's not it either, huh? (*Removes books.*) Well, what could "It" be?

Hippie (*Enters with guitar*): HEY! Intergalactic Brother . . . I find joy and satisfaction in my music. (*Shouts.*) Hit it!

(*Play loud hard rock music for a few lines.* **Hippie** *really gets down . . . then cut.*)

Hippie: Man, that's just gotta be "It"!

Betty: Randy, do you think that's got peace, pureness, and wealth?

Randy: No . . . I'm sorry, mister. But I don't think that's "It."

Hippie: Suit yourself. But (*Play rock music as he exits*) if that ain't "It," I ain't where "It's" at. (*Exits.*)

Betty: He might be right about that last statement.

Randy: Betty, I got it . . . "It's" . . .

Betty: Yes . . .

Randy: "It's" *money!* (*Rain monopoly money.*) All the world is always after it, so it must mean happiness; and you can buy all the warmth you need!

Betty: No, no, no! Money isn't good or fulfilling . . . or pure!

Randy: Well, phooey!!! Gimme another clue.

Betty: OK. "It's" not of this world.

Randy: You mean it's a spaceship? (*Antennaes or spaceship enter.*)

Betty (*Scared*): No, no! Don't say anything like that. Think, Randy . . . What's good? I mean really good?

Randy: Hmmm.

Betty: What's *pure*—totally *holy?*

Randy: Uh, I'm trying.

Betty: Randy, who is love?

Randy: Oh, that's easy. Jesus is Love.

Betty: Right! Exactly! (*Excited.*) That's "IT"!

Randy: Huh?

Betty: *Jesus* is good, *Jesus* is pure. *He's* peace, love, joy, smiles, warmth, meaning, happiness, satisfaction—*all* those things!

Randy: Hey, Jesus is "IT"!

Betty: YEA!

Randy: Well, since Jesus Christ is "It," then being a Christian is where "It's" at. We better go find our hippie friend and let him in on it.

Betty: Okey Dokey, my friend! (*They exit.*)

Good Ole Teacher

by W. H. Voorhes and Joey

V: Hello, everyone, how are you today? And good morning to you, Joey. How are you?

J: I'm tired.

V: Tired? What have you been doing to make you so tired?

J: School!

V: But, Joey, I thought you liked school.

J: Oh, I do summertime.

V: Some of the time?

J: That's not what I said.

V: What did you say, then?

J: I said I like school *summertime!*

V: Summertime?

J: Yeah.

V: But, Joey, school's closed in the summertime.

J (*Laughs*): That's what I like about school—summertime!

V: Joey, shame on you!

J: I was just kidding.

V: I certainly hope so. Seriously, now, what do you really like about school?

J: Good ole teacher, she was a lifesaver for me last year.

V: How was that?

J: Well, all year we colored every day.

V: Yes, most nursery schools do a lot of coloring.

J: Some days I was not very nice, and so I would mess up my coloring.

V: Joey, you didn't!

J: Yeah, I did.

V: Don't you know you should do your best work in school all the time, no matter what you're doing?

J: Now I know. I learned, 'cause good ole teacher saved me.

V: What do you mean she "saved" you?

J: Well, all our colorings were put in a big folder each day, and at the end of the year she said she was going to show them all to the folks.

V: Uh-oh.

J: Yeah, that's what I said. I was ashamed for not doing it right all the time, and I was afraid for the folks to see what I had done wrong.

V: I'll bet you were. What happened when the folks saw your messy colorings?

J: They didn't see them.

V: Why not?

J: Good ole teacher took all the messy ones away.

V: Wasn't that nice of her, Joey? Do you realize that Jesus is like that?

J: He is?

V: Yes, sometimes we do bad things which are called sins—it makes God unhappy to see us sin. But Jesus came to show us how to please God and how to make him happy. Then Jesus gave his life on the cross because that was a way for him to take all the bad things out of our lives. And everyone, if we tell God we're sorry for the sin in our life and ask him to let Jesus come into our hearts—Jesus will come in and take away all our sin—all the bad things in our lives.

J: Isn't that nice of Jesus? He must love us a lot.

V: He does, Joey; Jesus loves us very much. Everyone, Jesus loves you and wants you to love him and let him take away your sin. Let's bow our heads and close our eyes and ask him to come into our hearts. (*Prayer.*)

Don't Interrupt Me, I'm Praying

by Kenneth E. Walters

Petros: Well, that finishes our class for today. Thomas, will you lead us in prayer?

Thomas: "Our Father, which art in heaven."

Shalom (*Breaking right in*): Aaah, Thomas, you always pray like that.

Thomas: Don't interrupt me. Can't you see I'm praying? "Our Father, which art in heaven . . ."

Mary: Yeah, Thomas, what do you mean by that?

Thomas: I-I-I don't know. I was . . . you know, uh, just saying my prayers. It makes me feel good. It's . . . It's like getting my duty done.

Shalom: Well, if that's the way you feel, then go on.

Thomas: Let's see, where was I? Hmmmm, "Hallowed be thy name . . ."

Mary: Wait! What do you mean by that?

Thomas: It means . . . It means . . . Good grief, I don't know what it means. How should I know? It's just part of the prayer. Petros, what does it mean?

Petros: Hallowed means honored, holy, or wonderful.

Thomas: Hey, that makes sense. I never thought about that before. Let me go on. "Thy kingdom come, thy will be done on earth as it is in heaven."

Mary: Well . . . What are you doing to make God's will be done on earth?

Thomas: Nothing, I guess . . . I just thought that it would be neat if God was in control of everything down here.

Shalom: Does God have control of you?

Thomas: Weeeelll . . . I-I-I go to church. I even take my Bible sometimes. I read my Sunday School lesson one time last month.

Petros: But Thomas, you have to let God control your bad habits, your temper, the way you talk about others, your language, your—

Thomas (*Breaking in*): Will you guys stop picking on me! I'm just as good as some of the rest of those phonies at the church.

Shalom: But Thomas, I thought you were praying for God's will to be done. If that is to happen, it will have to start with folks like you and me.

Thomas: Oh well, I guess I do have some hang-ups, now that you mention it.

Mary: Yeah! Let me name a few. You have a terrible . . .

Thomas: Wait! Hold on a minute! I know what I am! Let me finish praying. This is taking a lot longer than usual. "Give us this day our daily bread . . ."

Mary: You need to cut down on the bread. You are overweight as it is.

Thomas: What is this? "Criticize Thomas Day"? Here I am doing my religious duty and you keep interrupting me. Can't you see I'm praying?

Petros: Praying is a dangerous thing. It can change your life! Don't stop now, Thomas, this is getting very interesting.

Thomas: Well, OK. But I wish you guys would stop interrupting me. "Forgive us our debts, as we forgive our debtors."

Mary: What about Bill?

Thomas: I knew that you would interrupt me again, Mary. I knew that you would bring him up! But he has told lies about me and got me in a whole bunch of trouble.

Shalom: But your prayer—what about it?

Thomas: I didn't mean it . . . I mean, I-I, uh, uh, I mean not that part of it.

Petros: Well, at least you are honest. But you are not comfortable with that much bitterness in you, are you?

Thomas: No! But I'll feel better when I get even with Bill. Boy, have I got some plans for him.

Shalom: You should forgive Bill. Then the hate and sin will be his problems. Then you will feel better.

Thomas: I'm not sure that is the best way. Boy, I would like to get even with him. I'll, I'll . . . (*Voice fading.*) but . . . all right! I'll forgive Bill. He's probably so miserable. Anyone who acts as he does is not with it . . . .

Don't interrupt me . . . let me finish my prayer. "And lead us not into temptation, but deliver us from evil."

Mary: Am I glad to hear you say that! Just don't go places where you will be tempted.

Thomas: What do you mean by that?

Shalom: Quit hanging around with those boys who cuss all the time. They are always bragging about "popping pills," "smoking joints," and just everything! They say they are having fun, but they don't know what life really is.

Thomas: Yeah, I get the message, loud and clear. Ten-four, good buddy. Let me finish my prayer. "For thine is the kingdom, and the power, and the glory forever. Amen." (*All four join in singing, "Let's Just Praise the Lord."*)

(Adapted from "After this Manner Pray," *Campers on Mission Newsletter*, November 1975, Home Mission Board, SBC, 1350 Spring St., Atlanta, GA. 30309)

Yes, No, and Wait and See!

by Marianne Hawkins

(**Susie** *enters alone, but does not speak. In a few moments,* **Johnnie** *enters and crosses over to her.*)

Johnnie: What are you doing, Susie?

Susie: Aw, nothing much. I was just thinking about something.

Johnnie: What, Susie? I didn't know you ever thought about anything!

Susie (*Shocked*): Well!

Johnnie: You know I'm just teasing, Susie.

Susie: Well, I hope so!

Johnnie (*Chuckles*): Really, Susie, were you thinking about something important?

Susie: Yeah, Johnnie. I was just thinking about prayer.

Johnnie (*Nods head*): That is important!

Susie: Well, what I was wondering is—Why doesn't God give us everything we pray for?

Johnnie (*Pauses slightly*): Well, maybe God just doesn't think we need everything we pray for.
Susie: Well, I know, but if God loves us, he should give us what we want.
Johnnie (*Scratches head*): OK, Susie, let me see if I can explain it like this. Suppose your baby sister saw a sharp, shiny knife and cried for it. Would you give it to her?
Susie: Of course not, silly! She would hurt herself!
Johnnie: But Susie, don't you love your little sister?
Susie: Sure I do. But I don't want her to get hurt.
Johnnie: I know! And because you love her, you wouldn't give her that old knife to hurt her. You wouldn't give her anything that wasn't good for her. God is like that, too. Sometimes he just has to say no when we pray for things we don't need.
Susie: Hey, now I think I understand what you mean!
Johnnie: And suppose it was a bright, sunny day and you asked your mom if you could play outside or go to the park. What would she say?
Susie: She would say yes like God says yes to our prayers sometimes!

Johnnie: Yeah—and sometimes he says "Wait and see."
Susie: Wait and see? What do you mean?
Johnnie: Yes, Susie. God sometimes tells us to wait and see. Like if you asked your mom to take you skating next weekend, or something like that.
Susie: Oh, now I get it. She would say, "Wait and see."
Johnnie: God gives us those three answers, too. Yes, no, and wait and see. He always listens to our prayers. Even though we don't always understand, God loves us very much and wants the things that are best for us.
Susie: You're right, Johnnie. I understand so much better now. Thanks for helping me!
Johnnie: You're welcome, Susie. Glad I could help. Hey, let's go play in the park.
Susie: OK! But I have to go tell my mom where I am going. I'll race you to my house!
Johnnie: You'll never beat me! Let's go! (*They exit.*)

Reprinted from *Puppets for a Purpose,* Evangelism Supply and Publications, Inc., Nashville, Tn., © copyright 1974. Used by permission.

The Puppet

by Steve Phillips

Mike (*Enters hurriedly*): Rudy! Hey, Rudy, you here?
Rudy (*Behind curtain*): Be there in a minute.
Mike: Hurry.
Rudy (*Enters*): Hi, Mike. I'm glad you could come by.
Mike: John said you wanted to see me. What do you want?
Rudy: I was wondering if you'd like to play checkers with me tonight. We'll have lots of fun. That is, if you don't mind losing. (**Rudy** chuckles aside.)
Mike: Well, I'd like to, but I can't.
Rudy: How about monopoly? We could get into an all-night monopoly game.
Mike: I've got to . . .
Rudy: I know, I bet you want to just sit around and watch the game on TV tonight. I'll get Mom to make us some popcorn. How's that?
Mike: It sounds great, but I can't. You see, I'm supposed to go play basketball with Tommy tonight.
Rudy: Basketball! I love basketball! I was captain of the basketball team in puppet school.
Mike: You played basketball in puppet school? I didn't know they had a team in puppet school.
Rudy: Yeah, I'll show you. (**Rudy** exits, gets basketball, reenters.) Watch this! (*Tries to spin it on finger, it falls off.*) Well, it's been awhile.

Mike: That's pretty good. Well, listen, Tommy's waiting for me, so I'd better go.
Rudy: Hold on. I'll get my coat and we'll go together.
Mike: Wait. (*Pauses.*) Listen, Rudy. I'm afraid you can't.
Rudy: Can't. What do you mean?
Mike: Well, we're going to be playing hard, running up and down, and, well, you just can't.
Rudy: But why?
Mike: Because you're just a puppet. Puppets can't play with us. We like you a lot, but I'm afraid you just can't. I'm sorry.
Rudy (*Dejected*): Oh, that's OK. I understand. Maybe some other night we'll get together and do something.
Mike: Yeah, we'll do that. Well, I guess I'd better be getting on now.
Rudy: OK. See ya. (**Mike** exits.) See ya, Mike. (*Pauses, lays head on curtain.*) Just a puppet! I *can* do things like people. I'll show them! Watch this. (*Exits, returns with cowboy hat on. Pretends to lasso, gets on a horse. Rides along, saying "getty up," then pantomimes horse throwing him off. Takes hat, tosses it off. Sulks on the curtain.*

Gets another idea. Exits and returns with baseball hat and glove. Says, "Batter up." Pantomimes throwing a pitch, watches ball sail over his head. Tosses hat and gloves back.

Thinks, exits, returns with sunglasses on. Slicks back hair. Sticks thumbs up like the Fonz, says "Hey!" Realizes this won't do either, throws sunglasses back.

Sits for a while. Suddenly gets brilliant idea. Hey, wait a minute. (*Exits, returns with Bible. Turns pages.*) Where is that Scripture? (*Turns pages.*) Here it is. I can do all things through Christ who strengthens me. I can do anything with Christ helping me. I can do things people can't do. Watch this. (*Pushes face together, then opens mouth real wide, waves his hands, pulls his head up, twists it around and down.*) Yeah, I can do lots of things. With God's help, I can do lots of neat stuff. I can't wait to tell the guys. Hey, Mike! (*Exits.*)

Incident at the Grand Canyon

by Tom deGraaf

Willie (*Enters with stick and cowboy hat*): Wow! The Grand Canyon! This thing must be at least ten miles deep! Hey, what's that down there? . . . That looks like Mom and Sally riding a mule train down into the Canyon! Yep! That's them, all right. Mom has her saddle on backward, and Sally's mule is completely hysterical. Hi, Mom! Hi, Sally! (*Voice echoes.*) Outta sight! An echo! I'm gonna try that again! Hi, Mom! Hi, Sally! (*Echoes again.*) This is terrific! Let's see . . . What else can I say? Maybe something witty . . . (*Thinks.*) Hey! There's a great big lizard over there! (*Rushes to it.*) Hmmmmm . . . looks like a Gila Monster to me. I wonder if he's friendly? (*Sticks finger near it; a ferocious growling is heard.*) Growl at me, will you? Take that! (*Klunks lizard with stick, watches it fall over edge into Canyon–hits with a crash.*) Take that, Godzilla! (*Echoes . . .* **Willie** *is elated.*) I just love that echo! Hello, down there! (*Echoes.*) Hello, Grand Canyon! (*Echoes.*) Hello, rocks and trees! (*Echoes.*) Hello, river! (*Echoes.*) Hello, Gila Monster! (*Instead of echo, a growl comes back–***Willie** *is momentarily startled.*) My mom is pretty! (*Echoes.*) My sister Sally stinks! (*Echoes twice. He laughs–doesn't see* **Dad** *enter, yells again.*) Dad golfs like a rookie! (*Echo waits momentarily.*)

Dad: And what are you doing, son? Enjoying the Canyon?

Willie (*Startled*): Why, nothing, Dad! (*Echo–"Dad golfs like a rookie . . . and your son Willie told me to say that."*) Hee hee . . . Sorry about that, Dad.

Dad: I see you're having a good time with the echo.

Willie (*Excited*): Yeah, Dad! That echo is the neatest thing I've ever heard! . . . (*Moody.*) I sure wish I could take it back home with me.

Dad: Why's that?

Willie: Well, it's kind of fun. It says just what I want it to. (*Brightens.*) And it agrees with me about Sally!

Dad: Willie, did you ever stop to think that you hear echoes all the time, wherever you go?

Willie: What do you mean by that? I don't get it.

Dad: Yell down to the Canyon again and say, "I don't like you!"

Willie: I don't like you! (*Echoes.*)

Dad: Now yell out, "I love you!"

Willie: I love you! (*Echoes.*) So what's that prove?

Dad: Well, Willie, all of us go through life hearing echoes. If we are saying by our words and actions that we don't like other people, those people will echo the same feelings right back to us. On the other hand, if we are constantly saying that we love others, they will echo love and kind words back to us.

Willie: I love you! (*Echoes.*) I see what you mean, Dad. If I say kind things to others, they'll say kind things to me!

Dad: That's right, Willie. Your life and my life are echoes of what we are inside . . . Hey! Why don't you go back to the car and get us a couple of Cokes and sandwiches and meet over there at that picnic table. I think your mom made us some peanut butter and banana sandwiches for lunch.

Willie: Right, Dad! (*Starts to exit, stops.*) Oh, here's my stick, Dad. (*Gives stick to* **Dad.**)

Dad: What's this for?

Willie: Just in case Godzilla comes back. (*Growl is heard.*)

Dad: Right! Now go get those sandwiches. (**Willie** *exits.* **Dad** *starts to go, stops, yells.*) Hello down there! (*Echoes.*) It's lunchtime! (*Echoes.*) I hate peanut butter and banana sandwiches! (*Instead of echo, his wife answers from below. "I heard that, dear, and you are in big trouble!"* **Dad** *is startled, drops his stick and runs off, yells.*) Bye, everybody! (*Echoes.*)

It's Love

by J. B. Collingsworth

Anna (*Sings happily*): It's love, it's love, it's love that makes the world go round. It's love, it's . . .

Mary Kathryn (*Interrupts, very tacky*): Oh, be quiet! You're so gushy! You—you—almost make me ill.

Anna: Hey, what did I do wrong? What's the matter?

Mary Kathryn: The whole world is what's wrong. I'm sick of seeing all of the poverty, hatred, hypocrisy, and political junk. You're so plastic, Anna—singing (*Sarcastically*) "It's love, it's love that makes the world go round."

Anna: Well, it's true! It *is* love—real love. God's kind of love. There's nothing plastic about that. Nothing can match it—nothing can take it away!

Mary Kathryn: Oh, yes—the world can take it away. I'm tired of all of the things that I see. It's time we did something about it.

Anna: Oh, but we are doing something about it. Just last summer on our mission trip, remember? (**Mary Kathryn** *shakes head no.*) Oh, that's right, you didn't go. Well, what about our new mission church; you've helped out there, haven't you? There are so many needs. (**Mary Kathryn**
shakes head no.) Well, you have been in on some of our projects such as going to take food to needy families, going to the nursing homes, and giving parties, and going to the children's homes and playing with the kids, haven't you? (**Mary Kathryn** *drops eyes, slowly shakes head no.*)

Anna: Where have you been?

Mary Kathryn: Oh, I come to Sunday School; but I'm so busy—I have band practice; I'm in the school play; plus I'm on the tennis team, and I just got elected to the student council. I have class to go to, of course. I just run myself ragged doing everything.

Anna: Well, maybe we've found the problem.

Mary Kathryn: I think—well—I think we have too! God's not number 1 in my life. I can't worry about the world and its problems if my life isn't right and if I'm not doing my part right here in (*name of town*). God's love does make the world go around. I've just been holding back. Thanks to you, though, it's going to change! Come on, let's go get a cola and talk some more. (*They exit.*)

The First Youth Choir Tour

by Tom de Graaf

Willie (*Excited*): Can you believe it, Cool Charlie?! Our youth choir is finally going on tour! I'll be famous!

Cool: That is so far out that even I, the coolest guy in our youth department, still can't believe it!

Willie: Where do you think we'll go on tour?

Cool: I haven't heard yet. Nobody's said.

Willie: Well, why don't we decide? We could map out this whole tour and then, when my dad asks us, we'll already have it planned!

Cool: Good thinkin'. Now, the way I see it, the first place we should hit is San Francisco. Yeah! All the top groups play there. San Francisco!

Willie: Far out, Cool Charlie! I'll have to get me some new shades and platform shoes . . . get my hair done!

Cool: OK, the second place we hit is Aspen, Colorado. I figure maybe John Denver could sit in and play guitar for our youth choir . . . Maybe sing a little too!

Willie (*Ecstatic*): That is so cool that only you, the Cool Charlie, could have thought of it!

Cool: Right, Willie. Now, I think our next stop should be in . . .

Sally (*Enters*): Hi, Cool Charlie. Hi, Willie. What are you guys doing?

Cool: Me and your brother here are plannin' out our youth choir tour. We're gonna be stars!

Sally: Oh, isn't it exciting? I never thought our youth choir could ever go on a tour!

Willie: Well don't get your hopes up 'cause you can't go. With you on stage, we haven't got a chance.

Sally: Oh, yeah? How come, smart mouth?

Willie: For one thing, your breath is what's destroying the Ozone layer.

Sally: Humph!

Willie: Face it, Sally, you just aren't show material like Cool Charlie and me.

Sally: That's not true! I am just as neat and professional as any of the big stars. As a matter of fact, last week at the junior swimming meet, I turned quite a few heads!

Willie: As I remember, it was more like quite a few stomachs.

Sally: I'm going to tell Dad on you, Willie! (*She exits.*)

Cool: Man, your sister is bad P.R. . . . What are we going to do with her? You know she'll come along.

Willie: Aw, don't worry about her, Cool Charlie. We'll let her unload the bus and stuff like that while we are signing autographs.

Cool: Good idea. Now, the next place we ought to sing at is Madison Square Garden in New York . . . I mean if the Beatles did a benefit concert there, it's the least we could do . . . Uh oh . . .

Dad (*Enters with* **Sally**, *eyes them. Boys look at each other, sensing impending doom*): Hi, boys. Having a good time? (*Glares at* **Willie**.)

Willie (*Shaken*): Uh . . . I don't know, Dad. Hey, Cool Charlie, are we having a good time?

Cool (*Frightened*): Uh . . . I don't know either. How good of a time were we supposed to be havin', Mr. Weekers?

Dad: Not that good, boys. Sally said you were making fun of her . . . something to the effect that she couldn't go on the youth choir tour.

Willie: Oh . . . yeah. Maybe we did say something to that effect.

Sally: They sure did, Dad. What are you going to do about it? I hope you make 'em stay home. Make 'em stay home, OK, Dad? Please? Make 'em both stay home from the choir tour!

Dad: Calm down, Sally, I'll handle this. Now, explain what's going on here, boys.

Willie: Aw Dad, Cool Charlie and I were just tryin' to plan out our youth choir tour.

Cool: Yeah, Mr. Weekers. We're already planning to sing in San Francisco and Colorado!

Willie: With John Denver!

Dad: Ummmhmm . . . And what about your sister here? Are you going to do all this without her?

Willie: Well . . . Cool Charlie and I are going to be big stars on account of this tour. But if Sally goes along and sings, we won't get to first base. You know that her Brother (Minister of Music) lets her sing in church once a month just to run the rats out of the attic. I mean many a church mouse has lost his religion over her voice.

Sally: That's not true! My voice has the characteristics and flow of Olivia Newton-John!

Cool: You got part of it right.

Dad: Boys, I think we have a serious problem here, and we need to face it.

Willie: Right, Dad! It's my career that's at stake!

Cool: Not to mention my "Cool."

Dad: Boys, I'm really disappointed in you. Don't you have the slightest idea about the purpose for a choir tour?

Willie (*Thinks*): Well, I wanna be a star . . . Uh, Cool Charlie wants to sing with John Denver . . . And (boy and girl in church) want to hold hands on the bus. I guess that about covers it.

    (**Sally** *throws up hand in despair, exits.*)

Dad: Willie, Cool Charlie, those aren't very good reasons for going on a choir tour.

Willie: They're not?

Cool: What if I get Elton John to play for us?

Dad: Sorry, but this choir tour is far more important than just a lark-in-the-park sort of deal. You'll probably be singing for some people who are experiencing some deep problems and hurts. There will be people who don't have friends or anyone who loves them.

Willie: Are you trying to tell us that Sally *is* going?

Dad: I'm trying to tell you how important your tour can be for all the people that hear you. And do you remember the three things God—not Elton or John Denver—but three things God asks us to do in this life?

Cool: No . . .

Willie: I forgot.

Dad: God asks us, you and me, to do three things to make our lives and the lives of others happier and fulfilled: First, to glorify him; second, to grow in Christlikeness; and third, to show those you meet how to trust in Jesus for salvation and true freedom. Do you know what?

Cool: What, Mr. Weekers?

Dad: You have a chance to do all three of those things on your youth choir tour. You can do all three of the things God has asked you to do. Does that sound important to you?

Willie: You're right, Dad. I guess San Francisco and my platforms will have to wait.

Cool: Yeah . . . I guess John Denver will have to get along without me. Mr. Weekers?

Dad: Yes, Cool Charlie?

Cool: I suppose Sally can come along too. She's not really that bad a singer. Maybe I could give her some tips . . . You know . . . like how to throw the microphone into the air and catch it on your knees! . . . Stuff like that.

Willie: Hey, Dad, I'm sorry we were so hot on making ourselves big stars. Besides, with the musical our group is doing, we'd probably mess it up by acting far out. We're gonna really try hard to make this tour worthwhile to our audiences, to ourselves, and to God! Thanks for the advice, Dad. I guess we did sort of get carried away there for a moment.

Cool: Yeah, thanks, Mr. Weekers. I don't know how I forgot to include God in our tour. That wasn't what you call *cool* . . .

Dad: Sure, guys.

Sally (*Enters dressed as rock star*): Hey, boys, get a load of me—Sally Tenille!

(**W & C** *look at each other in amazement.*)

Sally: You know, like in the "Captain and Tenille"! (*Jive-sings "Love will keep us together."*) Well, guys, do I get to go on youth choir tour now?

(**W & C** *look at each other again.*)

Willie (*Takes* **Sally**'s *arm*): Uh, Sally, this isn't what we do on choir tour.

Cool (*Takes other arm*): Uh, no, Sally. We don't do any of that jive stuff on youth choir tour because we're supposed to be singing our witness for the Man. (*Looks upward.*)

Willie: That's right, Sally. We're not foolin' around on this trip 'cause we're singin' for God's glory.

Sally: Does that mean my silver-glitter platform shoes are out?

Willie: I think me and Cool Charlie here need to fill you in on some things, my misguided sister. (*They exit.*)

Dad (*To audience*): You know, they're gonna do just fine on that tour now . . . just fine. (*Exits.*)

I Miss My Grandmother

by Jim Stewart

(**Gerdie** *enters, sulking, head down.*)

Bert: (*Enters*): Gee whiz, Gerdie, why the sad clown act?

Gerdie: Oh, I'd rather not say, Bert.

Bert: Aw, Gerdie, you're making the whole world look sad. Why don't you tell ol' Bert what's wrong? You know they don't call me man's best friend for nothing!

Gerdie: You wouldn't understand, Bert. It's a very personal thing and . . . besides, I'm afraid you'd laugh. And since when do you think you are man's best friend? That's supposed to be a dog, not a puppet!

Bert: Whoever started that rumor just didn't know about puppets. Why, I understand humans better sometimes than they understand themselves.

Gerdie: Well, I'm not a human. I'm a puppet, and I don't want to talk about this anymore.

Bert: OK, be miserable! If you turn down my offer to help, then there's nothing more I can do.

Gerdie: All right, all right, all right! I'll tell you; but if you laugh, so help me, Bert, I'll never speak to you again, as long as I live.

Bert: Just try me and calm down, so I can understand you.

Gerdie: OK, here goes. You see . . . uh : . . um . . . well . . . I have a problem.

Bert: Well, I never would have guessed! I know that, silly, just tell me what it is!

Gerdie: Well, I miss my grandmother! That's it. I finally said it.

Bert: Gerdie, you're going to have to be a little more specific than that.

Gerdie: I'll try. You see, my grandmother has always been like another mother to me. I mean, we're really close.

Bert: So what's the problem?

Gerdie: Well, since my dad took this new job and our family has moved, Grandmother and I are miles and miles apart, and I can't see or talk to her regularly, like I used to. Now, Bert, don't you dare laugh at that.

Bert: I'm not laughing. I was just thinking about something.

Gerdie: Well, tell me what it is. I want to know what you think about my problem.

Bert: Do you really want to know what I think?

Gerdie: Of course! I almost swallowed my tongue, trying to get it out in the first place. Now what is going through your boyish mind?

Bert: Well, I think you're a very lucky girl. That's what I think!

Gerdie: Lucky? Here I've poured out my despair to you and you have the nerve to tell me that I'm lucky? Of all the nerve! You insensitive, inconsiderate . . .

Bert (*Interrupts* **Gerdie**): Just hold on a minute and let me explain.

Gerdie: Well, your explanation had better be good, or I'll see that you never counsel any of my puppet friends ever again!

Bert: Gerdie, you ought to stop feeling sorry for yourself.

Gerdie: Says who?

Bert: Says me—because a lot of kids like me see their grandparents all the time, yet hardly realize they're there.

Gerdie: I don't understand.

Bert: What I'm trying to say is that you evidently have a really unique relationship with your grandmother, something I've never had with mine. I envy you.

Gerdie: Well, Bert, why couldn't you have the same kind of closeness with your grandparents?

Bert: Oh, I could have, but I didn't. My grandparents are miles away now too, but I don't even think about it because I never really got to know them during the years we lived only six blocks away.

Gerdie: Gee, Bert, I'm sorry. I just didn't realize . . .

Bert: It's all right, Gerdie. You didn't know it; but in telling me your problem, you've helped me with one of mine.

Gerdie: How's that?

Bert: Well, I'm going home right now, and call my grandparents and tell them I love them. And then I'm gonna . . .

Gerdie: Bert, wait a minute. What about my problem?

Bert: Oh, I think you ought to go visiting.

Gerdie: Visiting? What kind of an answer is that?

Bert: A very good one! You may be miles away from your own grandmother, but there are plenty of someone else's grandmothers in our town, who could stand some of the love you have to give. You won't be betraying your own grandmother because she would probably be happy to know that you're spreading a little love into the life of someone else. Besides, doesn't the Bible sort of teach that the more love you give away, the more you have to give?

Gerdie: Yeah, something like that.

Bert: Well, when you do get to see your own grandmother, you'll appreciate her even more.

Gerdie: I'm beginning to see what you mean. Sort of like being a temporary grandmother to someone else's grandmother?

Bert: Yeah, you're catching on. It won't be hard to find a substitute grandmother.

Gerdie: Sure, maybe I can find one in a rest home where there are some grandparents who seldom get to see their own families.

Bert: Right you are!

Gerdie: Gee, Bert, how can I ever thank you enough for helping me with my problem?

Bert: You need not thank me. After all, you uncovered an area of my life where I'm lacking.

Gerdie: What do you say we both go to a rest home and find some new friends?

Bert: I think we're already here!

A Friend Is a Gift You Give Yourself

by J. B. Collingsworth

Alexander: Hey, man, how're you doing?

Thomas (*Stunned*): Super, I guess . . . uh, do I know you?

Alexander: Well, kind of. I met you once and I've seen you lots of times.

Thomas: You have got a good memory. I wish I could remember that well.

Alexander: Remembering isn't the trick. I really did wish that we could become friends, but I never did reach out to you to try to be a friend. I guess you could say that I was afraid of being rejected.

Thomas: Come to think of it, now I do remember a girl who knew both of us telling me that she thought we had a lot in common. It's coming to me now. I guess we both felt that way. I never really got to know you either.

Alexander: Yes, that happens often. I'm a Christian, but often I really miss the boat. I don't reach out to people because I'm afraid they may not like me. Do you feel that way?

Thomas: Sure! I suppose we all do.

Alexander: Well, since we both see it the same way, let's spend some time together really becoming friends—and I'm speaking of really talking, sharing, and becoming brothers.

Thomas: Hey! That sounds super! You know, I once heard someone say, "A friend is a gift you give yourself." So . . . I accept you as my friend right now! How about it?

Alexander: That's great. I'm touched. I really don't know what to say.

Thomas: Alexander, don't you think that we should tell everyone to stop and look at the gifts?

Alexander: Gifts? What gifts?

Thomas: Those you were just talking about. The gifts all around us. First you take the bow and ribbon off, all the paper and tape, and then open the package and find inside a beautiful Christian friend.

Alexander: You're OK, Thomas. You're OK. (*Puppets embrace, exit.*)

The Brick Wall

by Steve Phillips

Narrator: Once there was a man named Birney. (**Birney** *enters.*) And a man named Bill. (**Bill** *enters.*) Birney and Bill were the very best of friends. (**Birney** *and* **Bill** *turn to each other, stick their tongues out, make terrible noises at each other.*) Well, most of the time they were best friends.

Birney: You're not my friend.

Bill: You're not my friend either.

Narrator: This wasn't one of the times they were best friends. You see, Birney had made Bill real mad, and Bill had made Birney real mad.

Birney: You make me sick.

Bill: You're a nerd.

Narrator: What made this so bad was that they lived next door to each other. Finally Birney thought of something.

Birney: Hey, I've just thought of something.

Bill: That's a change.

Birney: I can't stand looking at you, so I'm going to build a brick wall ten feet high. That way I won't have to look at you.

Bill: That's fine. Because I don't want to look at you either.

Birney: The only trouble is that I don't have enough mortar.

Bill: I have plenty. I'll be glad to let you borrow some. I'd build it myself, but I don't have enough bricks.

Birney: I have plenty of bricks; do you want some?

Bill: Sure. I'll let you have some of my mortar if you'll let me borrow some of your bricks. In fact, we can work together to build this wall.

Birney: Hey, that's a great idea. When can we start on it?

Bill: I have to mow my grass first. And with my lawnmower it might take all night.

Birney: Why don't you use my mower? It's a lot faster. I've got to make some shelves for my wife. And my saw is worn out.

Bill: I have a sharp saw. Just use mine. Then we can start building the wall sooner.

Birney: Are you sure you don't mind?

Bill: I don't mind at all.

    (**Birney** *and* **Bill** *exit.*)

Narrator: So Bill and Birney did all the things they needed to do. After a while, they came back together. (*They enter.*)

Bill: I'm through.

Birney: Me too. Are you ready to start on the wall?

Bill: Yes. Let's get started.

Birney: Hey, wait a minute.

Bill: What is it?

Birney: I can't remember why we were going to build the wall. Do you remember?

Bill: Sure. It was because . . . well, we wanted to . . . to tell you the truth, I don't remember either.

Birney: Well, we don't need to build it then.

Bill: We sure don't. How about playing tennis with me?

Birney: I'd love to. If I can borrow a racquet.

Bill: Sure. I just bought a new one. You can use it, and I'll use my old one. I'll be over in a few minutes.

Birney: See you then.

    (**Birney** *and* **Bill** *exit.*)

Narrator: So Birney and Bill forgot about building the wall because best friends don't need walls between them.

Let's Be Honest

by Steve Phillips and Donna Kirkpatrick

(**Roosevelt,** *in glasses, and* **Fred,** *with hat on, enter.*)

Roose: Hey, Fred, I've been reading this book that says that when other people ask us questions, we should answer them honestly.

Fred: Oh, I agree.

Roose: I mean perfectly honest. No little white lies to make the other person feel better.

Fred: Man, I think you've really hit the groove.

Roose: And I think we should be like that. If I ask you a question, I want you to give me what's really on your mind.

Fred: And I want you to do likewise.

Roose: Man, I feel better already.

Fred: Me too. I feel like I've turned over a new lily pad.

Roose: Hey, how about going bike riding? I want to try out my new speedometer.

Fred: Well . . .

Roose: Remember, be perfectly honest.

Fred: Well, I really don't feel like riding bikes just now. Do you mind?

Roose: Not a bit. You were just being honest.

Fred: Isn't it neat to be perfectly honest?

Roose: It sure is.

Fred: Hey, speaking of being honest, don't you honestly love my hat?

Roose: Well, if you want to know the truth . . .

Fred: Sure, lay it on.

Roose: I hate that hat!

Fred: What?

Roose: I think it looks terrible on you.

Fred: Everyone else tells me they love this hat on me.

Roose: I'm afraid they weren't being honest with you. You see, it makes your skin look putrid green.

Fred: You don't have to be so personal.

Roose: Well, we agreed to be honest.

Fred: If you want to be honest, I honestly hate those glasses. They make you look like a telephone pole with a concussion.

Roose: They do not.

Fred: They do too. I hate those glasses.

Roose: Well, I hate that hat!

Fred: Well, I think I'm going to leave.

Roose: Go right ahead. I don't care if I ever see you and that stupid hat again.

(**Fred** *exits, pauses.*)

Roose: Maybe I shouldn't have said that about Fred's hat. It's good to be honest with other people, but we shouldn't hurt their feelings. I'll find Fred and tell him I'm sorry.

Fred (*Enters*): Roosevelt.

Roose: Fred.

Fred: Roosevelt!

Roose: Fred!

Fred: Roosevelt?

Roose: Fred?

Both: I'm sorry.

I Need You Too

by Steve Phillips

Fred (*Enters, sees* **Roosevelt** *motionless*): Hello there. I'm Fred. The friendly neighborhood frog. What's your name? (*No answer.*) I live on the lily pad by the big rock. Where do you live? (*No answer.*) Can't you talk? (*No answer.*) Or are you just unfriendly? (*No answer.*) Talk! (*Sees something besie* **Roosevelt,** *reads it.*) Hey, what's this? It's a note. It says, "Push the button to make me talk." Push the button to make me talk? Oh well, it's worth a try. (*Pushes button.*)

Roose: Hello. My name is Roosevelt. I live at four-twelve Main Street.

Fred: Why didn't you talk when I first came up? (*Pauses, pushes button.*)

Roose: I can't speak unless you push the button. I need your help before I can talk.

Fred: You need me? Wow, somebody really needs me. (*Gets excited.*) You can't do anything without me. (*Gets cocky, laughs.*) You're totally dependent on me. Ha! Ha!

Sam (*Enters*): Hey, Roosevelt! Hey, Fred!

Fred: Hi, Sam. Hey, Sam, you know what? Roosevelt here can't talk or do anything unless I push this button. Isn't that great?

Sam (*Unimpressed*): That's fine, Fred, but I've got more important things to talk about.

Fred: Like what?

Sam: Well, Fred, I'm not accusing you, but my basketball is missing. And someone said they saw you going into my room. Now I don't really think you took it, but I was wondering if you had some proof you didn't.

Fred: Sure I have proof. I've been here with Roosevelt. He'll tell you that I couldn't have taken your basketball because I've been here with him. (*To* **Roosevelt.**) Tell him, Roosevelt. Oh, I almost forgot. (*Pushes button.*) Now tell him. (*No answer.*) Tell him. Come on. (*Still no answer.*) Hey, Roosevelt, quit playing around. (*Continues to try and make* **Roosevelt** *talk. After* **Fred** *gives up,* **Roosevelt** *speaks.*)

Roose: Fred didn't take your basketball. He's been here with me the whole time.

Sam: Thanks, Roosevelt. Fred, I didn't think you took it. I just had to make sure. (*Exits.*)

Fred: Hey, what's the big idea not telling Sam I'd been here?

Roose: You see, Fred, I need you, but you need me too.

Fred: I need you? How's that?

Roose: God wants us to depend on each other. You can do some things I can't do, but I can do some things you can't do. If we work together we'll both be better off. In Hebrews 10:24 the Bible says, "Let us be concerned with one another, to help one another, to show love, and to do good." We shouldn't feel superior over other people because we all have a part in God's plan.

Fred: Roosevelt, I'm sorry. You're right. We do need each other.

The Math Problem

by Ann Brandon

Ginger: What are you doing?

Herman: I'm trying to figure out a math problem.

Ginger: Homework?

Herman: No, I just heard a story in Sunday School about how many times Jesus said you should forgive someone. (*Pauses.*) I got it! Four hundred ninety times!

Ginger: Herman, Jesus didn't say it quite like that.

Herman: Well, almost. Peter asked him how many times he should forgive someone, and Jesus said 70 times 7. And that equals 490.

Ginger: Now wait a minute, Herman. What are you doing now?

Herman: I'm figuring out how many times I've forgiven my friends. Boy, it sure is going to take a long time to get up to 490. It's really going to be hard to keep track of all of them.

Ginger: Herman, that's the point! Four hundred ninety sounds like a lot of times, and it is, and it's hard to remember a lot of things.

Herman: I don't get it.

Ginger: Jesus just used that as an example to say that we should forgive people all of the time and not keep count of how many times we do it.

Herman: I get it—forgive them and then don't worry about it any more. And if they do something else, just keep forgiving them without keeping track of how many times you do it. Right?

Ginger: Right.

The Turned-over Wagon

by Karen Marcus

(*Props: Two small dolls, a wagon, card (posterboard) with verse printed on it, sign for Sunday School class.*)

Carol (*With wagon and doll*): Miiilllllllddddd-dddrrreeedddd!

Mildred: What do you want?

Carol: Can you come out and play with me? I have a brand-new doll, and I want to take her for a ride in the wagon. You bring Thumbelina, and they can ride together.

Mildred: Just a minute and I'll ask my mom. (*Exits calling mother.*) Moooo—oooom! Oh, Mom! (**Carol** *plays with doll, arranges dress, and so forth.* **Mildred** *returns carrying doll.*)

Carol: You can let Thumbelina ride first . . . We always let company be first.

(*Girls arrange dolls in wagon; a third puppet enters. He dashes in, turns wagon over, bends over with laugher. Girls rescue dolls.*)

Mildred: Carl Yates! You are the meanest person on earth!

Carl (*Stops laughing*): Ah, gee, I was only joking.

Carol: That wasn't very nice!

Carl: I'm sorry. Can I pull the wagon and give your dolls a ride?

Mildred: No! Not after what you just did!

Carl (*Pleads*): But I said I was sorry.

Mildred: That doesn't matter. We don't like you!

Carl (*Yells*): Well, I don't like you either! (*Exits.*)

Carol: That wasn't very nice.

Mildred: He deserved it! (*Offstage voice calls* **Carol.**)

Carol: That's my mother calling for me to come home. I'll see you at church tomorrow.

Mildred: OK. Bye, Carol! (**Mildred'**s *mother calls also.*) That's my mother calling me too. Guess it's time for lunch. (*Exits.*)

(*Sign appears. It reads "Class 3 and 4." Puppets enter class.*)

Mrs. Ruth: Good morning, boys and girls! I'm so glad you came today. Let's start by singing our favorite song, "Jesus Loves the Little Children." (*Puppets join teacher in singing song.*) Isn't it good to know that Jesus loves each one of us? Jesus loves everyone. When he lived on earth, he also loved everyone. Sometimes people did not treat him nicely, but he did not become angry or fight back. Jesus told us that we should love God with all our hearts, souls, and minds. And he also said that we should love our neighbor as much as we loved ourselves. Who do you think our neighbor is? (**Carol** *raises hand.*) Carol.

Carol: Our neighbors are the people around us.

Mrs. Ruth: That's right, Carol. In the Bible we find a verse that tells us about this. And I have written it on this card.

(*Holds large card with Luke 6:31 on it.*) Let's read it together. "And as ye would that men should do to you, do ye also to them likewise." Luke 6:31. What does this mean? (**Carl** *raises hand.*) Carl.

Carl: If you want to be treated nice, you have to act nice.

Mrs. Ruth: That's right, and even if others are mean to you, you should be nice to them. There's a little song that we can learn to help us remember this verse. (*To tune of "On Top of Old Smokey."*) "Do unto others as they should do to you, O, do unto others as they should do to you." Now let's try it together. (*All sing together.*) Let's try to do that this week. Come back next Sunday and bring a friend.

(*All exit but* **Carol, Mildred,** *and* **Mrs. Ruth.**)

Carol (*Softly*): Mildred, we weren't very nice to Carl yesterday.

Mildred: No, we were not. We were not doing what the Bible verse said. What should we do?

Carol: Let's ask Mrs. Ruth. Mrs. Ruth, may we ask you something?

Mrs. Ruth: Of course, Carol, you know I'm your friend.

Carol: Yesterday, while we were playing, Carl turned our wagon over. He said that he was sorry, but then we still wouldn't let him play when he asked. Now we have decided that we didn't do the right thing. But what should we do?

Mrs. Ruth: When you can see that you did something wrong and you want to do something about it, you are acting very grown-up. What did Carl do when you told him that you didn't like the way he acted?

Mildred: He told us he was sorry. Gee, Carol. Do you think we could apologize?

Carol: We can try.

Mrs. Ruth: I am very proud of you girls.

Mildred: Let's go, Carol. (*They exit.*)

(**Carol, Mildred** *return.*)

Carl: He must be around here.

Mildred: Cccaaaarrrllll! (**Carl** *appears.*)

Carl: Here I am.

Carol: We're sorry for the way we acted yesterday. We shouldn't have been so mean.

Carl: I'm sorry, too, for the way I acted. I really didn't mean what I said.

Mildred: Let's go and get the wagon and take the dolls for a ride. We'll let you go first. (*They exit.*)

Once a Frog . . .

by Tom DeGraaf
(*Story line contributed by Denise Boisvert*)

Youth Director: Well, friends, here we are at the local lily pond covering a most interesting story. It seems that yesterday a mysterious flash of light was seen in this area, and I am here to check out the report. Hmmm . . . There seems to be no one here (**Frog** *appears*) except this miserable frog.

Frog: Hey, wait a minute buddy, I'm no frog. (*Croaks.*)

Youth Director: This is fantastic! A talking frog!

Frog: I told you before, I am not a frog. (*Croaks.*)

Youth Director: How did you learn to speak so well, Froggy?

Frog: For the last time, I am not a frog. I am really a human trapped in the body of a frog!

Youth Director: A human trapped in the body of a frog . . . right.

Frog: You see, I was walking home from school yesterday when I decided to take a dip in the lily pond. Well, I was swimming around here in my birthday suit when all of a sudden this old witch came along. She could see right off that I was a handsome guy and asked me for a little kiss. But I ducked under and came up across the pond from her. That burned her up pretty bad . . .

Youth Director: Are you trying to tell me a witch wanted to kiss a frog?

Frog: No! I was a handsome guy at the time! Human! (*Croaks.*) So I started laughin' at her and callin' her names from across the pond. I could see she was gettin' madder and madder, but I kept it up anyway. All of a sudden she yelled out "AbbaZaba" and this bolt of lightning hit me. That's when she turned me into a frog. (*Croaks.*)

Youth Director: So that's what the light was . . . Well, too bad, Froggy. See ya around. (*Starts to exit.*)

Frog: Hold it! Don't leave me like this! (*Buzzing sound is heard.* **Frog** *sees a fly, stalks it, catches it, eats it before realizing what he's done.*) Oh, yuk! I hate those things! (*Croaks.*) You've got to do something to help me!

Youth Director: OK. OK. But how do I know you're really a person inside that frog suit?

Frog: Ask me a question that only a human could know!

Youth Director: OK . . . Hmmm. What does . . . what does the "Y and R" stand for?

Frog: Y and R . . . "The Young and the Restless" soap opera!

Youth Director: You're human.

(**Frog** *croaks.*)

Youth Director: I have it! I know what you must do. You must go to that old witch, tell her that you're sorry for calling her names and making fun of her, and then give her a kiss.

Frog: Are you kidding? That witch has a mouth like a moray eel! (*Croaks.*)

Youth Director: Well, if you want to stay a frog the rest of your life, I guess that's your choice . . .

Frog: No. I guess you're right. I'd better go say I'm sorry for callin' her names. I'll make peace with her, and maybe she'll change me back into a human again. I really miss being my old handsome self.

Youth Director: Good. Now get going. (**Frog** *hops off.*) Well, I never would have believed it. I wonder what he really looks like . . .

Youth (*Stands up behind stage*): It worked! I'm wonderful me again! She changed me back!

Youth Director: She sure did! Making peace and apologies always works. Wow! You sure are handsome!

Youth: I know. (*Big smile and wave to audience; watches out for flying tomatoes, and so on.*)

Looking at a Christian

by Mary Lou Serratt

Sally (*Enters alone*): Let's see . . . short. No, that couldn't be right. Well, young . . . no. Old, then . . . no. Oh, I give up . . . I just can't figure this out!

Janie (*Enters quietly*): Hi, Sal!

Sally: Oh! You scared my hair straight! Where did you come from . . . and why are you bothering me? Can't you see I am busy! My Sunday School teacher asked me to write out what a Christian looks like. (**Patty** *enters.*) I just can't decide. At first I thought a Christian must be short, like Mr. Roberts, 'cause he is such a super-great Christian . . . he's always at church and he's so helpful to folks. Then I remembered Mr. Stein . . . he's such a good Christian the way he helps those kids that don't have a dad, and he gives a lot to mission work . . . but he's real tall!

Patty: You do have a problem, Sally. Wow, good thing I came along to help . . . uh, now, let's see . . . maybe you should say "A Christian is average in size." (*Proud of herself.*)

Janie: Sally, are you sure your teacher wanted to know what a Christian looked like?

Sally: I guess I ought to know! Now don't get me confused.

Patty: Oh, no, don't do that! So, now what?

Sally: Well, at first I thought a Christian would look old because Granny Lester is such a good Bible teacher. Then I decided no—young, like the choir director. Oh, I just give up.

Janie: Sally, I think maybe your teacher wanted to know your description of a Christian, right?

Sally: That's what I said!

Janie: No, Sally . . . that means what is a Christian really like, not just what he looks like. You've already decided that Christians all look different on the outside. It's what's on the inside that makes them special.

Patty: Oh, yeah, like we studied about the other day in the "be-attitudes."

Sally: Oh, say, thanks. I should have looked up the definition of "description," I guess. Oh, my, now I really don't know where to start!

Janie: Why not start with the Bible and get the answer straight from God? Matthew, chapter 5, gives a good description. Verse 2 begins with "Blessed . . ."

Patty: Oops, better get the dictionary out again!

Janie: Blessed means happy, remember? And that's one of the first things you can notice about a Christian.

Patty: That's right! All those people you've been talking about . . . aren't they happy people?

Sally: You know, that's right! They always seem to be happy. Even when Mr. Stein's house burned, he was saying that God was good to him because no one was injured. He was happy even then. And Mrs. Wear was even happy in the hospital with her broken hip. She said it gave her a chance to study her Bible more and to tell the people she met there about Jesus.

Janie: That's one important thing about a Christian. He believes that Scripture which says "All things work together for good to those that love the Lord." Jesus gives us a joy that nothing can take away. What else can you remember about all these great Christian people you've been thinking about?

Patty: I know! They all care about me and about each other, too. You know, like they help people and are friendly and seem to enjoy being together.

Janie: Another way to say that is . . . they love one another. That's how the first Christians were known. Folks said: "Behold, how they love one another."

Sally: Another thing is, they don't hold grudges and go around fussing about things. They always look for the best in other people.

78

Janie: Yes, and in doing that they are obeying Jesus. He tells us in Luke that we will be forgiven as we forgive each other. And also, we shouldn't act like we are better than anyone else.

Patty: Oh, these people never do that!

Sally: No, they make me feel so warm and loved and important. And they tell me things to help me be a better Christian, too.

Janie: I think you are getting a good description, Sally.

Sally: And you know, I can tell these people are good Christians because of what they do, not because of what they say about themselves. They don't go around with a sign saying, "Hey . . . I'm a Christian!" I just know they are Christians because of the way they live.

Patty: They are always doing kind, helpful things and letting Jesus show them how to live.

Janie: Yes, a growing Christian will show it by the way he lives.

Sally: I think I have it. "A Christian is happy, loving, forgiving, helpful, and tries to live as Jesus wants him to." That's my description of a Christian . . . isn't it a beautiful picture?

(**Janie, Patty** nod in agreement.)

Janie: You know . . . that gives us something to ask ourselves. (To audience.) How about it, folks—do you look like a Christian . . . on the inside?

(Follow with a discussion about the fruits of a Christian.)

Share Your Soda?

by Jeff Wyers

(Props: two soda bottles, three straws.)

Tony (Enters with soda bottles without straws): Beatrice? Bea Baby, where are you?

Bea (Offstage): Just a minute, Tony.

Tony (To audience): I just bought these two sodas, and I'm going to share one with my friend Beatrice if she'll ever get here—Beatrice!

Bea (Enters behind Tony): Boo!

Tony: Yahh!

Bea: Ha Ha—I scared you.

Tony: No you didn't; nothing scares me.

Bea: Very much—were you calling me?

Tony: Yes, I wanted to share my sodas with you.

Bea: Oh, Tony, that's so sweet. Wait just a second, let me run and get some straws. (Exits with bottles.)

Tony: Straws? But we don't need straws. (Banging sounds offstage.) Wow, she's making a lot of racket.

Elmer (Excited): What's going on; what's that? A stampede? The elephants have escaped the zoo? The Martians have landed? An earthquake? Tony, Tony, what's happening?

Tony: Relax, Elmer. It's just Beatrice looking for some straws.

Elmer: Straws? You mean like soda straws? I sure am thirsty.

Tony: Yeah, well, you can't have any of mine. You can get your own as far as I'm concerned.

Bea (Enters): Here we are. Oh, hi, Elmer.

Elmer: Hi, Bea.

Tony: What was all that noise down there? (Takes sip.)

Bea: Oh, I just had to dig around a little to find the straws. (Takes sip.) Elmer, would you like a sip?

Elmer: I sure would; I'm thirsty.

Tony: Hey!

Bea: Just a minute, let me get another straw. (Exits, gets straw, returns.) There. (**Elmer** takes a sip.)

Elmer: Thanks a lot, Beatrice. I really needed that. Well, I gotta go now. I gotta finish mowing the lawn now. I'll see you all later. Thanks again for the soda, Bea. (Exits.)

Tony: Why did you do that?

Bea: Do what?

Tony: Give him some of your soda. He coulda got his own.

Bea: Tony, you know better than that. Jesus said to love each other and to treat each other like we want to be treated—just like God treats us, with love.

Tony: Gosh, I didn't think of that. I guess I acted pretty selfish. I'll bet he's still thirsty. Let's go get him a soda of his own. Want to?

Bea: Sure. That's a great idea, Tony. Jesus would like that.

Tony: Elmer will too. (They exit.)

The Backstabber's Suite

by Jeff Wyers

(Beatrice *and* Elmer *are in front of Junk Store, beside "Disco Dance Hall."*)

Beatrice: Oh, Elmer, I just don't know what to get my boyfriend, Burford, for his birthday.

Elmer: Don't worry, Bea. I know just the thing. It's right here inside the Junk Store.

Beatrice: Are you sure it'll be right?

Elmer: Of course I'm sure. I told you I knew exactly what to get him and exactly where to find it.

(Mary *enters, watches* Elmer *grab* Bea's *hand.*)

Elmer: C'mon, Bea, stop standing there worrying. Let me show it to you.

Beatrice: Tee-hee. I'm so excited! I really love you for this. (*Exit.*)

Mary (*To audience*): Whooeee! Have I got a story! (*Exits running.*)

(*Music plays,* Mary *enters, whispers to* Leroy. *Next she whispers to* Philbert.)

Narrator: Mary had a little tale
    As juicy as can be.
And if you had an open ear,
    She'd tell you it for free.

She took it with her everywhere
    And passed it round the town.
It never came to mind that it
    Would bring somebody down.

She stretched the truth and twisted things
    Till they were out of whack.
But everyone she told it to
    Accepted it as fact.

It grew and changed and began to stink
    Of soured tongues and lies.
'Cause everybody added some
    To give their friends a rise.

Leroy: Did you hear about Elmer and Beatrice?

Philbert: Isn't that awful?

Leroy: It's sure something. Beatrice running around town with Elmer. What's Burford going to do?

Philbert: I don't know. Elmer has been his friend for a long time.

Leroy: Maybe that's why.

Philbert: Could be. You know, I heard they were holding hands.

Leroy: And I heard that she told him that she loved him.

Philbert: And they were headed to the Dance Hall.

Leroy: And they stopped and hugged and kissed!

Philbert: What?

Leroy: That's what I heard.

Philbert: Wow! I never.

Burford (*Enters*): Hi, guys. What's all the excitement about?

Leroy: You don't know?

Burford: What?

Philbert: About your girlfriend and your best friend.

Burford: Doing what?

Leroy: Running around on you!

Burford: What? No way! She's my girl and he's my best friend.

Leroy: So?

Philbert: Yeah, so?

Burford: So I don't believe it. Let me by.

(Leroy, Philbert *whisper, laugh.*)

Burford: You two had just better cut it out!

(Mary, *several others watch, laugh.*)

Burford: I mean it. You just better watch out about what all you're saying! They wouldn't do anything. (Desperately.) It's not true!

(Elmer *and* Beatrice *enter with package.*)

Beatrice: Burford, Burford! What's going on?

Burford (*Screams*): That's what I wanna know. Where've you two been? What have you been doing?

Elmer: What? We've been out . . .

Burford (*Cuts him off*): Yeah, I've heard. How'd you like a black eye? (*Starts for him.*)

Beatrice: Burford, Burford! Listen! We were getting you a birthday present.

Burford: What?

Elmer: Yeah. Here.

Burford: Oh, wow! I'm so sorry I flew off the handle.

Beatrice: That's OK. I guess it could've looked strange.

Elmer: Yeah.

Burford: What I wanna know is who started this? (*Looks at* Leroy, *who looks at* Philbert, *who looks at* Mary. *Everyone follows gaze, looks at* Mary. *All silent, then a puppet with tongue:* "PLLTTTZZZ!!!" Mary *screams, exits, followed by all except* Bea, Burford, *and* Elmer.)

Burford: I'm really sorry, you know.

Elmer: It's all right. Let's go open the present.

Beatrice: Yeah. Let's go.

Burford: You mean you forgive me for not trusting you, for getting mad at you?

Beatrice: Sure, Burford, that's what God taught us to do.

Elmer: Yeah, Jesus taught us to love one another even when we make mistakes. C'mon, let's forget it and go open the present.

All: Yeah, OK. That sounds good. (*Exit.*)

Narrator: It doesn't always work this way,
A sad fact but it's true.
Just remember all the pain that gossip
makes

May well return to you.

(**Mary** *enters screaming, looks around. Puppet appears beside her. She screams, heads left. Puppet appears. Screams, heads backstage. Puppet appears—puppets close in on* **Mary**—*all disappear at once—crash.*)

You Don't Say

by Greg George

Joe (*As* **Herman** *enters*): Guess what, Herman?

Herman (*After a slight pause*): Uh, your brother is in jail.

Joe (*A little disgusted*): No!

Herman: Are you sure that's not it?

Joe (*Loud*): Herman!

Herman: Well, he sure is mean—real mean. And not only mean but ugly too—real ugly.

Joe: Herman, shut up, and guess again.

Herman: OK, let me see. (*Looks up and all around, thinking out loud and mumbling.*) I've got it! Your mother wears combat boots.

Joe (*Surprised*): How did you know?

Herman: Just a lucky guess.

Joe: Well, she does wear boots when the weather gets real cold, but that's not it. Guess again.

Herman: You're a spy and you're defecting and moving to Russia.

Joe: Ha! Ha! Come on now, think real hard.

Herman: If you're not moving to Russia, then I give up. Come on, Joe, tell me the big secret.

Joe: OK, but you've got to promise not to tell anyone.

Herman: Sure, sure, I promise.

Joe (*In a whisper*): Well, I was told by a very reliable source . . .

Herman (*Interrupting*): Wait! Hold it! Stop right there!

Joe: What's wrong, Herman?

Herman: Are you about to tell me some gossip?

Joe: No, man, I'm about to tell you what Mark did in Mrs. Teal's class yesterday.

Herman: What Mark did? You mean Mark Hall?

Joe (*More excited*): Yeah, that's the one. Well, I was told that Mark . . .

Herman (*Interrupting*): Joe, did you see what you're about to tell with your own eyes?

Joe: No, but Jimmy's cousin, Johnny, said Jerry Burns told him.

Herman: Oh, brother, that's gossip and hearsay, Joe. You shouldn't spread rumors and gossip; that can be very damaging.

Joe: Damaging? Who would it damage?

Herman: First of all, you could be spreading something that may not be true, especially if you didn't see it take place yourself. And secondly, it could be damaging to you.

Joe (*Shocked*): To me! How?

Herman: It's like this: If you continue to spread gossip and rumors, pretty soon no one will want to be your friend because they can't trust you.

Joe: Gee, I never thought about it like that.

Herman: That's what happens with far too many people. They don't think about what they say.

Joe: What if it's something good about a person?

Herman: That's different. If you want to share something good, then everybody benefits. People begin to see you as a loving person who is always sharing good news about people; and that is the kind of friend most people want.

Joe: Yeah, I see—kinda like, "Do unto others as you would have them do unto you," huh?

Herman: That's right. Now, what was it you wanted to tell me about Mark Hall?

Joe: You know, I can't for the life of me remember what it was.

Herman: You don't say. Well, let's go have a cola and celebrate your loss of memory. (*Both exit.*)

I Love Me

by Judy R. Martin

Silas (*Talks or sings while playing with some toys*):
> I love me,
> Yes sir-ee,
> I love the way I look.
> I love the way I cook.
> I love the way I am so fair,
> The way I brush my wooly hair.
> I love the way I act and speak.
> I love the way I am so sweet!
> I love me!

Celia (*Enters*): Hi, Silas.

Silas: Hello. (*In a singing way.*) Don't you just love the way I greet you? Hello—

Celia: It is very nice. By the way, do you notice anything different? (*Turns around.*)

Silas: Uh . . . oh, you brushed your teeth?

Celia: No, guess again.

Silas: Uh . . . oh . . . you . . . oh . . . ah . .

Celia: Oh, Silas, it is my hair!

Silas: Your hair?

Celia: Yes, I combed it just for you . . .

Silas: Oh, of course it is nice, but I could have done it better. I am so artistic, you know.

Celia (*Sadly*): Of course you could.

Silas: I have to go. You know I am so popular. I have a million club meetings to attend.

Celia: (*Sadly*): Of course you do.

Silas (*To audience*): Bye . . . byeee. Don't you just love the way I say good-bye? (*Repeats.*) Bye . . . byeee. (*Exits.*)

Celia: Every time I do something Silas says (*Mocking Silas*) "I can do it better" or "Well, I would not have done it that way, but it looks almost OK" or "Maybe I could make it better for you." I am getting disgusted. I wish Silas would like something I do. I know; I'll put a ribbon in my hair. He will like that. (*Exits.*)

Silas (*Entering, to audience*): Oh, hi there. It is wonderful me again. I hope you are enjoying my act. It is too bad everyone isn't as good as me. (**Celia** *enters with ribbon in her hair.*) Hi, Miss Celia. Oh, my, there is something in your hair. May I get it out for you? (**Celia** *pushes him away, starts to cry.*) What is wrong?

Celia: I put this ribbon in my hair just for you. You like yourself so much you don't care about anyone else.

Silas: But . . .

Celia: I don't even want to be friends with you. Good-bye! (*Exits.*)

Silas (*Sadly*): Oh dear, I didn't realize how mean I have become. I only thought of myself. I didn't care about anyone but me . . . I thought I was the best. I didn't know it was possible, but I made a big mistake! Celia . . . Celia . . . Celia!

Celia (*Enters with nose in air*): What do *you* want?

Silas: I wanted to apologize for thinking only of myself. I really do think your ribbon looks nice.

Celia (*Sniffs*): You really mean it?

Silas: Of course. I even want to share my toys with you. How about it? Will you be my friend?

Celia: You really have changed! Yes, I will be your friend.

Silas: Good . . . let's go play with my toys. (*They exit.*)

Me First

by Rick Brown

(*In classroom.*)

Helen: Boys and girls, time for a drink of water!

Danny: Me first, me first.

Helen: OK, Danny, but be very quiet in the hall. (**Danny** *exits.*)

Chip (*To* **Frank**): He's always first.

Frank: Yeah! He must be the teacher's pet. What do you think, Judy?

Judy: Oh! It's fine with me.

Chip: But you're always last.

Judy: Well, that's not so bad. I still get my drink of water.

Frank: It's not fair.

> (**Danny** *reenters.*)

(*On playground.*)

Helen: Boys and girls, now we're going to see who can throw the ball the farthest.

Danny: Me first, me first.

Frank: Not again!

Chip: (*Bitterly*): Of course, why not?

Frank: Judy, don't just stand there; do something.

Judy: Like what?

Frank: Like . . . steal the ball away from Danny.

Judy: That wouldn't be very nice.

Chip: Well, he's not very nice either.

(*In cafeteria.*)

Helen: Line up for lunch.

Danny: Me first, me—

Chip & Danny (*Interrupt and yell*): First!

Helen: Boys, we'll have no yelling in the cafeteria. To the back of the line!

Chip (*Grumbling*): Doesn't he gripe you, Judy?

Judy: No, not really.

Frank: Why are you so different?

Judy: Last summer at Vacation Bible School, we learned a verse that says, "And whosoever will be the first shall be last." And the last, first. Jesus said that.

Chip: Who said that?

Judy: Jesus. He came to serve us and die for us and we should be willing to do the same for anyone, even Danny.

Frank: I guess we've got a long way to grow—I mean, go.

Judy: You're right. We've all got a long way to grow and go. Let's begin by putting God first in our lives and not ourselves.

(**Chip** and **Frank** nod in agreement.)

How's Your Love-Self?

by Sally Whittington

Puppet 1: Oh! Boo Hoʻ! Oh, sob! Just look at this stringy hair. (*Shakes head.*) Ugh! And these freckles. Gross! And what's worse, I'm dumb. When they passed out brains, I thought they said 'rain" and ran for cover. And I can't *do* anything! Whoever said "Everybody has a talent" never heard of me. I'd throw myself in the ocean and get it over with, except that I'm such a mess, I'd pollute it worse than the Nantucket oil spill! Oh, Boo hoo! Oh, no! Here comes somebody. (*Puts sack on head.*)

Puppet 2 (*Frog or green puppet, enters whistling*): Oh, hi, Abigail, what's happening?

Puppet 1: Not much.

Puppet 2. Say, that's a new paper sack, isn't it? What are you hiding today? Is it your ears again?

Puppet 1: No! It's these freckles! (*Rips off sack.*) Just look at . . . say, you've got freckles too.

Puppet 2 (*Brightly*): I sure do! And not just on my nose either. They're all over, see? (*Turns around.*) I just praise the Lord for these nice warts—or freckles, as you call them. You know, he put a lot of time and thought into creating me. If he had made me, say, red and smooth, the bugs I like to eat could see me very plainly, and I'd have an awful time catching them for lunch. And all those people who would love to eat my legs could spot me a mile away. Yep! I'd be hungry and legless if the Lord hadn't made me green and bumpy so I'd fit right in with the lily pads and bushes. Each one of us has a special purpose in God's creation, and he shapes us to fit that special purpose.

Puppet 1: Wow. Oh, no! (*Searches frantically for sack.*) Help me get this sack back on; my hair's the pits today, and here comes Miss America. (**Puppet 2** *exits.*)

Puppet 3: Hi, Abigail, I almost didn't recognize you without your sack. Oh, your hair looks so nice. You know, I used to think I'd be the happiest person in the world if I could wear my hair like that. But with my curly hair, it's just impossible.

Puppet 1: Really? But your hair is so neat; I'd give anything . . .

Puppet 3: But when I became a Christian, God's Holy Spirit showed me that I was putting too much emphasis on the outer person, and not enough on the inner person. Beauty is only skin deep. God knew what was important when he gave his son a human body, and it wasn't a handsome face or curly hair. You see, 1 Samuel 16:7 sums it all up—"for the Lord seeth not as a man seeth; for man looketh on the outward appearance, but the Lord looketh on the heart." We can't change our looks, but we can grow more beautiful on the inside, with God's help. (*Exits.*)

Puppet 1: Wow! Good grief! Where's my sack? Here comes the "Big Brain." She heard me ask that really dumb question in Algebra today. Maybe she won't notice me . . .

Puppet 4 (*Enters with book, wearing glasses*): $2+8x_2+15=0$, so $x^2+8x+15$ is $x^2+8x=15$. Hmm. (*Looks up.*) Oh, hi, homo sapien. Where's your sack today, Abigail?

Puppet 1: I wish I knew.

Puppet 4: Look, I noticed you were having trouble factoring in Algebra today. Would you like for me to help you with it?

Puppet 1: Groan!

Puppet 4: Then maybe you could help me with my crocheting. My granny squares always turn out round.

Puppet 1: You're kidding!! But granny squares are so easy, and you're so brainy.

Puppet 4: Look. God made us all different. My being good at Algebra, and chemistry, and literature, and history, and trigonometry, and biology, and . . . where was I? Oh. Anyway, my being good at these things doesn't make me any better than you, who can crochet a mean granny square. You see, God, in his great wisdom, made us proficient in different ways. If everybody was a whiz at Algebra, who would write the poetry, who would paint beautiful pictures, who would crochet granny squares? I thank God for giving me a good mind, and I ask him every day to help me use my mind for his glory. This verse from Proverbs helps me keep my eyes on him. "The fear of the Lord is the beginning of knowledge." But I sure wish I could crochet a granny square. (*Exits shaking head.*)

Puppet 1: Wow! Oh, here comes Crazylegs again!

Puppet 5 (*Jogs up*): One, two, one, two. Screech! Hi. Say, you look different today, Abigail. (*Walks around her.*) Oh, I know. You don't have your sack on!

Puppet 1: Yeah. And it's a good thing! You're standing on it. You still training for the Olympics?

Puppet 5: That's right.

Puppet 1: I ran one hundred yards in only five minutes in P.E. today. The teacher said I'm really improving.

Puppet 5: Great. You know, when I first became a Christian, I decided to give up my running and find another way to serve the Lord. But through prayer, I came to realize that God gives every talent, and he expects every talent to be used for his glory. And it can be, too. God has shown me opportunities to witness for him to people who might not ever set foot in church or roast a marshmallow at a youth fellowship. Everytime I do my best, or am a good sport, or am a good loser, I glorify his name. Here's one of my favorite verses—"But they that wait upon the Lord shall renew their strength. They shall mount up with wings as eagles, they shall run and not be weary, they shall walk and not faint." (*Exits.*)

Puppet 1: Wow! I never thought of that before!

Puppet 6 (Dog puppet): Look! I've been listening to this conversation. Abigail, you're a Christian, aren't you?

Puppet 1: Yes, but what does that have to do with . . .

Puppet 6: Well, the Bible says . . .

Puppet 1: More Scripture, eh? Well I can quote Scripture too, ya know. Listen to this: "Oh, wretched man that I am . . ." That's from Romans 7.

Puppet 6: I know how you feel. We humans are never satisfied with ourselves. I used to cry myself to sleep because I did not look like Lassie. But if we really believe God is in control, then we have to believe he was in control when he created each one of us. Right? Each one of us is a special, important piece in God's big puzzle; and no one, *no one*, can fill our spot as well as we can! There are so many Scriptures that tell us how special each of us is to God and to the body of Christ. Here's one from Psalm 139: "I will praise thee; for I am fearfully and wonderfully made; marvelous are thy works; and that my soul knoweth right well."

Puppet 1: Wow, I never realized I was knocking God when I knocked one of his great creations—*me, the eighth wonder of the world.* I won't need this anymore! (*Throws up pieces of sack.*)

All Puppets (*Sing to tune of "Jesus Loves Me"*): Jesus made us all different, that you can so plainly see, but he loves us all the same, he loves you and he loves me. Yes, Jesus loves us, yes, Jesus loves us, yes, Jesus loves us, the Bible tells us so.

God Made Me Special

by Randall Bardin

(**Mother** *is busily working*—**Gary** *storms through.*)

Mother: Hi, Gary. What's wrong?

Gary (*Disgusted*): Nothing!

Mother: Well, for nothing to be wrong, you surely seem upset. You look like you could cloud up and rain at any minute.

Gary: Well, if you'd just dropped the fly ball that could have won the ballgame, you'd be upset too.

Mother: Oh, I see.

Gary: And as usual, Bobby was his outstanding super muscle self. He struck out six batters and batted in three runs. That big showoff!

Mother: Wait a minute. You don't make your record any better by putting down someone else.

Gary: Well, why can't I play ball as well as Bobby? Why don't I do anything right? I'm not worth anything! (*Sobs.*)

Mother: Do you mean that my special son, with some special abilities and a special personality, is going to go around feeling sorry for himself just because he can't play softball as well as someone else? Come here to me, you big mess. Look out that window. Do you see the oak tree over there crying because he doesn't have any big beautiful flowers on its branches?

Gary: No . . . of course not.

Mother: Well, what's he doing?

Gary: He's just standing there, making shade like he's supposed to.

Mother: And is that honeybee crying into a tissue because it can't bark and carry the evening paper in to its master?

Gary (*Laughing*): Naw, Mom, he's carrying some nectar back to the hive so he can make some honey.

Mother: And Gary, do you remember when we looked at the big snowfall that came last winter? There wasn't one little snowflake that was exactly like any other snowflake. Were they upset? I should say not. They knew that they were the only snowflake in the whole world with their exact pattern.

Gary: But Mom, I'm not a snowflake. And I'm sure not as big as that giant oak tree.

Mother: That's right. But just like that snowflake, God has made you just in the pattern that he wanted. There's only one you in this whole world. Therefore, you're very special to God since you're the only you in the world.

Gary: OK. But why didn't God make me able to catch fly balls like Bobby?

Mother: Well . . .

Gary (*Interrupting*): and hit home runs . . .

Mother: Gary . . .

Gary: and run as fast as other guys can . . .

Mother: Are you finished?

Gary: Yes ma'am.

Mother: God has created you in a special way and at the same time given you special gifts and abilities that may or may not be like the abilities he's given other boys.

Gary: What do you mean?

Mother: What boy did you have to help with his science every afternoon this past semester?

Gary: Well, Bobby, but . . .

Mother: And who won the outstanding science student award at the assembly this spring?

Gary: You know it was me . . . (*Pauses.*) Oh, I get it.

Mother: Gary, you have something special to give back to God that no one else has to give . . . your life. And the best part is that you're special to God because he has chosen to love you. He proved he loved you when he let his own Son come to live and die and be raised from the dead for you.

Gary: Thanks, Mom. I feel a lot better now. (*She exits. He turns to look in a mirror and sings a song about how God has made him special and how God's love is special to him.*)

No Longer a Schmeil

by Tom deGraaf

(*The stage has a steering wheel at one end, so that it becomes the scene of a car interior.*)

Dad (*Enters, grabs wheel*): Hey, Willie, Sally, come on and get into the car. Let's go have some lunch.

Willie: Coming, Dad! (*They enter, line up behind Dad as if in car.*) Lay some rubber, Dad.

Dad: Close the car door, Sally. Put on your seat belt.

Sally (*Pulls imaginary door shut*): OK, Dad. Let's go! (*Sound of car taking off is heard. Dad drives for about thirty seconds, having several near-accidents, none of which they seem to notice or react to.*)

Dad (*Still driving*): Well kids, wasn't that a great sermon we heard today? Too bad your mother was sick and had to stay home from church.

Willie: At least the roast won't be burned.

(**Sally** *suddenly bursts into tears.* **Dad** *is startled, swerves car, skids to stop.*)

Dad: Sally! You nearly scared me to death! I could have had a terrible accident!

Willie (*Looking back*): You did! You just wiped out a fire hydrant and two beagles.

Sally (*Still crying loudly*): Daddy, I'm a . . . a schmeil!

Dad (*Looks back*): I hit a what?

Sally (*More upset*): Daddy! Listen to me! I said I'm a schmeil! (*Continues crying.*)

Willie: So who's arguing? Dad, we'd better get the car off the curb.

Sally (*Builds to climax*): Will somebody please listen to me? (*All is quiet.*)

Dad: Why, Sally . . . dear . . . why are you so upset? (*Puts arm around her.*)

Willie: Yeah, why? Dad's hit fire plugs before . . .

Sally (*Sobbing quietly*): I . . . it was the sermon today at church. It made me feel bad.

Dad: The sermon made you feel bad?

Sally (*Nods*): Yes.

Dad: Willie, you go turn off the water at the hydrant and apologize to those beagles. Tell 'em there's another one down the street.

Willie: Right, Dad. (*Exits.*)

Dad: Now, dear, tell me exactly what's bothering you. What was it in the sermon that made you feel bad?

Sally: I don't have a gift! (*Cries again.*)

Dad: What? What did you say?

Sally (*Grabs him*): A gift. I don't have a spiritual gift like the preacher said! (*Lets go, cries.*)

Dad: OK, Sally. I think I understand the problem and am ready to talk about it. But first, you're going to have to stop . . . crying.

Sally (*Stops crying immediately*): OK, Daddy.

Dad: Now. I think you misunderstood what the preacher was saying this morning about spiritual gifts.

Sally: No, I didn't. He said that every Christian has a certain spiritual gift and that we should find out what it is. Now am I right or not?

Dad: You're right, Sally. I guess you understood that part.

Sally: Well, the preacher is still wrong. I don't have a spiritual gift. I have looked and looked, and as far as I can tell I'm still as inept as I ever was.

Dad: Sally, let me remind you that 1 Peter 4:10 says, "As each has received a gift, employ it for one another, as good stewards of God's varied grace." That verse says that if you are a Christian, as you are, you have been given a spiritual gift by God to be shared with others.

Sally (*Distraught*): But what gift have I been given?

Dad: OK, Sally. I want you to listen carefully because I'm going to tell you in two minutes what the preacher said in today's forty-five-minute sermon.

Willie (*Enters*): . . . Everything's fine, Dad. I got the water turned off at the fire hydrant. The two beagles gave me a bad time, though. One stole my shoe.

Dad: Good, son. Now as I was about to say, Sally, you have a spiritual gift that is different from any natural abilities you might have been born with. A natural gift is like the ability to speak well or be a good cheerleader. But a spiritual gift is a gift from the Holy Spirit to you so that he can minister through you to other people. In other words, the Holy Spirit wants to be able to use you, to work through you. So he gives you a gift. You and he use that gift to minister to other people.

Willie: What kind of gift are you talking about?

Dad: Well, there are several kinds of gifts. The Holy Spirit might give you the gift of preaching, or teaching, or soul-winning, or administering, or ministering to people in a physical way. He may also give you the gift of faith, giving, mercy, wisdom, healing, or others.

Sally: But what gift do I have?

Willie: Yeah, what gift does Sally have?

Dad: Don't worry about that. You'll find out. When God gives you something, he'll make sure you know what it is and how to use it.

Willie: I don't know, Dad . . . Sally's been a schmeil for a long time how. Maybe there's been a slip-up.

Sal (*Indignant*): And I suppose you have it all figured out, Willie? (*Looks down.*) . . . You can't even keep track of your own shoes.

Willie: I told you. The dogs got it.

Dad: Kids, the main thing to remember is that as we discover our spiritual gifts, we must be willing to let the Holy Spirit minister through us by way of that gift.

Sally: I got it! I just got it! The beauty of the whole thing is that the gift is God's direct channel through us to others! It's the only way that the Holy Spirit can speak through us to other people!

Dad: Sally! That's marvelous! That was tremendous the way you just put it all together like that!

Sally (*Embarrassed*): Aw, it was nothing, Dad. Actually, I just happened to remember it from what the preacher said this morning.

Willie: Dad? Do you think I have a spiritual gift too?

Dad: Sure, Willie. All Christians do. We say we can feel the Holy Spirit when the preacher preaches because that's the way the Spirit works through him. Or we feel the Spirit through the music because the music director is using his gift to let the Spirit come through to us.

Sally: That's so simple now! And it's beautiful!

Willie: It sure is, Dad. Thanks for explaining it.

Sally: Now I know I'm not just an inept schmeil. I'm a gifted person.

Dad: That's right, Sally, and do you know what gift I think you have?

Sally: What, Daddy? What gift do I have?

Dad: I think you have the gift of faith and vision, Sally. I think you have the spiritual ability to let others see God in you by keeping after something, no matter how difficult, until you find it! People will be uplifted by you, Sally, because the Holy Spirit can speak through you to them as you tackle the tough and difficult problems in life.

Willie: What about me, Dad? What's my gift? What's mine?

Sally (*Venturingly*): Turning off fire hydrants!

Dad: Not quite, Sally. I don't think that was on the list. (*To Willie.*) Let's me and you talk about that just as soon as we get home. OK, son?

Willie: Right, Dad. (**Dad** *takes wheel again.*) Do a wheelie, Dad! Do a wheelie! (*The car takes off, and they leave in a cloud of dust.*)

Post-Basketball Game

by Tom deGraaf

(**Willie** *and* **Cool Charlie** *enter with white towels around their necks.* **Willie** *carries small basketball.*)

Willie: Whew! Cool Charlie, that was absolutely the worst our basketball team has ever been beaten . . . 250 to 3! I mean, the other team made so many baskets that after the first quarter our cheerleaders went home . . .

Cool Charlie: This really looks bad for the Cool Charlie's image, man. And it's all your sister Sally's fault too. We should have never let her join our basketball team—especially as coach!

Willie: You're right, Cool Charlie. She has no ability at all to coach a basketball team. Did you notice that once during a time-out she wasn't even there at the bench to talk to us?

Cool Charlie: I know . . . I spotted her in the stands laughing it up with the boys in the Pep Band.

Willie: Not exactly standard coaching procedures.

Cool Charlie: It's her fault that we lost the game! She is the most incompetent person I've ever seen. Did you know that before the game I saw her connecting the dots in our basketball play books?

Willie: She's got to go. That's all there is to it! I mean, here we are, terrific basketball stars, and we have to play for a hair-brained female who half the time substitutes the water boy by mistake . . .

Dad (*Enters carrying basketball banner*): Hi, Willie—Hi, Cool Charlie. You boys sure did your best out there on the court today. Try not to feel too bad about losing, though. It was only your first game.

Willie: You mean our last! The principal was so embarrassed we got beat that he canceled the rest of the season and rented the gym out to a dog show promoter.

Dad (*Consoling*): Well, try not to take it too hard. It's not your fault because both of you really do have a great talent for basketball.

Cool Charlie: The problem is that Sally doesn't! She has ruined the Cool Charlie image so bad that the pom-pom girls won't even speak to me anymore. After today's game they'll be calling me on the phone just so they can hang up.

Willie (*Throws down basketball in disgust*): My sister Sally is a nitwit! I've always wanted to play basketball in the worst way, and sure enough—Sally showed me how.

Dad: OK, hold it a minute, son. I think we'd better talk this thing over before it gets any worse. Now, you boys have been trying to tell me that Sally is imcompetent, incapable, and . . .

Willie (*Interrupts*): Obnoxious!

Dad: Willie! Now—as I was saying—yes, boys, you seem to feel that Sally has no abilities whatsoever. Is that correct?

Cool Charlie: You have a gift for understatement, Mr. Weekers.

Dad: I think I have to agree that Sally is not your best basketball coach.

C & W: Right on! Now you're talkin'!

Dad: But that is not to say she doesn't have other abilities that may be just as important.

Willie: What do you mean, Dad?

Dad: Well, just yesterday I saw your sister Sally doing the dishes and cleaning the house.

Cool Charlie: So?

Dad: So Sally has the ability to be helpful and handy around the house. You guys know how she's always helping Mom.

Willie: Yeah . . . and Mom's nearly a basket case . . .

Dad: Well, just as you boys have the ability to play basketball, Sally has the ability to be a good and thoughtful helper to her mother.

Willie (*Not impressed*): Aw, anybody can put a few dishes in a dishwasher—That's no hard job.

Dad: I seem to remember that it was you who did the dishes once and put them accidentally into the garbage compactor. Those dishes were totaled.

Cool Charlie: Nice going, Klutza! Probably had water spots too.

Dad: The Bible says that all of us have different abilities according to our blessing from God. It says that in Romans 12:6.

Willie: Romans 12:6. What's the verse?

Dad: It says, "Every man has a different gift, according to the grace given to him, for service to God." Grace means God's love and blessing.

Cool: You mean God has blessed all of us with a gift or ability?

Dad: Yes, he has!

Willie: Even in Sally's case?

Dad: That's right.

Willie: Are you sure?

Dad: Of course. Now the point of this whole discussion is that you must learn to respect the gifts of others. But the problem still remains that Sally has not yet realized her gift of being a helper. She doesn't know how to use it right.

Cool Charlie: Mr. Weekers, I have just come up with a good way to use Sally's gift of helping, and at the same time save our basketball team and gym from the dog show promoters.

Dad: How?

Cool Charlie: First, we'll ask the principal if we can have one more basketball game to try and redeem ourselves. Then we'll convince Sally that as a good coach and helper, she must sit in the stands right behind the other team's bench!

Willie: What good will that do? She'll still be in the same gym with us, even if she is sitting behind the other team's bench.

Cool Charlie: I know! But we'll convince Sally that the best way to help our team, and thereby exercise her gift of helping, will be to sit behind the other team and aggravate them to tears!

Willie: Right on, Cool Charlie! They'll be so aggravated by her that they won't know what's going on in the game!

Cool Charlie: And all Sally has to do is be herself!

(*They look at* **Dad** *for approval.*)

Dad (*Shakes head slowly*): Sorry, boys. That's not a very good idea.

Willie: Don't you think it will work, Dad? Don't you think it will work?

Dad: Oh I'm sure it'll work, all right. But you boys still don't seem to understand that this verse means more than just using your own abilities. It means that you should use your abilities for God.

Cool Charlie: I guess you're right, Mr. Weekers.

Willie: Yeah, you're right, Dad. I guess we should just be thankful for our own gifts and not worry about other people's.

Dad: That's right, Willie. Tell you what . . . if you boys will promise to put some of your athletic abilities to work for God and help me with the youth snow retreat at church next week, I'll promise to talk to Sally about staying out of the gym.

Willie (*Excited*): Do you really mean it, Dad?

Dad: Yes, son.

Cool Charlie: Wow! Thanks, Mr. Weekers! We'd really appreciate it a lot!

Willie: Come on, Cool Charlie! Let's go start planning the church snow trip, and then practice some basketball! (*They exit excited.*)

Dad (*To audience*): Well, I'm glad those boys have learned to use their athletic abilities for God. Now if I can only get Sally to see how to better use hers by helping other people . . . and by staying out of the gym!

Cool Charlie (*Reenters*): Uh, Mr. Weekers, could you get her to stay out of the locker room too? I mean, helping is helping . . . (*Confidentially.*) But her handing out towels? (*They exit.*)

Mowers and Frogs

by Randall Bardin

Dad: Michael!

Mike: Yes, Dad?

Dad: Where's your brother?

Mike: Right behind me, Dad.

Tommy (*Enters*): Whew! If it gets any hotter today I think I'll melt like a popsicle. What'd ya want, Dad?

Dad: I'm leaving to go to the barbershop; and while I'm gone I want you boys to mow the yard and trim the hedge. I'll be gone for a couple of hours, so you have plenty of time to do a good job. OK?

Mike: Consider it done, Dad.

Dad: I'll see you boys later—don't forget to pick up the trash out of the yard before you mow! (*Exits.*)

Tommy: Right, Dad! Come on, Mike, let's get started so we can get finished.

Mike: OK, I'll mow and you can clip the bushes.

(**Ricky** *enters.*)

Tommy: I'll bet I can beat you to the tool shed!

Ricky: Hi, guys.

Mike: Hi ya, Ricky!

Tommy: Hi, Rick, whatcha' doin'?

Ricky: A bunch of the guys are goin' down to the river to catch frogs to throw over the fence at Mary Ellen Smith's tea party! Come on! (*Exits.*)

Mike: Oh, boy! (*Starts to exit.*)

Tommy: Hey, Mike, are you forgettin'? We've gotta do the yard.

Mike: Are you kiddin'? I wouldn't miss this for the world! I'll mow the yard when I get back. (*Exits.*)

Tommy: OK, but I hope you make it before Dad gets home. Oh, well, guess I better get started on those bushes. (*Exits, humming.*)

(*Later that afternoon . . .*)

Dad: Boys, I'm home—Tommy, Michael . . .

Tommy: Hi, Dad!

Dad: Where's Mike?

Tommy: Well, Dad, ya see, he uh . . .

Mike (*Enters*): Oh, hi, Dad—you're home.

Dad: Did you boys finish the yard?

Tommy: The bushes are all cleaned and trimmed!

Dad: Good. Did you mow, Mike?

Mike: Well, uh, ya see, Dad, some of the guys came by and, uh, well, we sort of, um . . .

Dad: Did you mow the yard, Michael?

Mike: No, Dad, I was down at the river catching frogs.

Dad: I'm very sorry to hear that—you see, the reason I was gone so long was because I picked up some tickets for the baseball game tonight.

Tommy: Oh, boy!

Dad: But Mike, I'm afraid you won't have time to mow the yard before we leave, so I guess this time you'll have to stay home and finish the work you were supposed to do. Come on, Tommy, it's time to get ready for the game. (*Exits.*)

Tommy: Gee, Mike, I'm sorry you can't go.

Mike: Yeah, it just doesn't seem fair.

Tommy: I don't know, Mike. Remember the story we learned in Bible Study last week? How Jesus gave his disciples jobs to do, to go around helping people? So it would please him? I don't think mowing the yard is any less important for you and me to do than the jobs they did. And if we do the jobs given to us, then it pleases Jesus just as much.

Mike: Yeah, I guess you're right. Jesus must not be too happy with the way I acted today. So from now on I'm going to do my jobs right and when they're supposed to be done. Then Jesus, and Dad, and everybody will be happy!

Tommy: Come on—I'll help you get the lawn mower out! (*They exit.*)

The Lost Book

by Shirley B. Martin

(*Prop: box on stage to one side.*)

Ronald (*Enters, goes to box, looks around*): I know my book was here someplace. (*To audience.*) Did you see my book? I'm sure it was here. (*Looks again.*) It must be here. I knew it! My book is here, but it is under this box.

Wilber (*From under box*): Grrrrrrrrrrrrrrrr.

Ronald (*To audience*): Did you hear anything?

Wilber (*Under box*): Grrrrrrrrrrrrrrrrrrr.

Ronald (*Goes quickly to other side of stage to audience*): You must have heard that. I must think of something to do. I have to get that box off my book. (*Pauses.*) I know, I'll just push it off. (*Creeps over to box and pushes hard.*) Oh, my, it just doesn't want to move.

(**Wilber** *knocks on inside of box.*)

Ronald: What was that? (*Shakes all over.*) Oh . . . I'm . . . scared! (*Backs to the other side, pauses.*) I know; I will run over and lift it off. (*Runs over, tries to lift it.*)

Wilber (*Mysterious voice*): Whoooooooooooooooo is touching my box?

Ronald: It is haunted! (*Runs back to the other side.*) What am I going to do? (*Thinks.*) It looks like I will never get my book again. (*Pauses.*) I know! (*Goes over to box, tries to*

climb on it. Every time he tries, **Wilber** *moves box and tips him off. Finally, he tips the box so much that it falls off, revealing* **Wilber.**)

Ronald: Wilber!

Wilber: Did I scare you?

Ronald: You are not very nice.

Wilber: I just wanted to have some fun.

Ronald (*Mad*): That is no way to have fun.

Wilber: I'm sorry. I didn't mean to make you mad.

Ronald: You never think how you might make other people feel when you do things.

Wilber: Please don't be mad.

Ronald: You will lose all your friends if you act like that.

Wilber: I said I'm sorry. Please forgive me.

Ronald: Well . . . are you going to scare me anymore?

Wilber: I promise I won't.

Ronald: Are you going to think first how your actions will make other people feel?

Wilber: I will.

Ronald: OK. Come on, we will go and share some cookies and milk together. (*Both exit.*)

King of the Jungle

by Steve Phillips

Narrator (*As* **Narrator** *talks,* **Lion** *enters*): Once upon a time, the animals in the jungle got together to elect the king of the jungle. The lion had always been the king, but he had been treating the other animals harshly, so they elected Mr. Rabbit as their new King. Naturally, the lion was heartbroken, so he went and poured his heart out.

Lion (*Cries tremendously*): Why me? Why me? I thought I was a good king.

Narrator: Just at that moment a boy was walking through the jungle, whistling away as he went. (*Boy enters, trying to whistle.*) Or at least he was trying to whistle. Suddenly he heard the lion crying.

Lion (*Terrible cry*): Oh, if only I was still the king.

John (*To audience*): Hey, there's a lion, and he's crying. (*To* **Lion**.) Hey, what's the matter?

Lion: Oh, I didn't know you were there.

John: What were you crying about?

Lion: Me crying? Have you ever seen a king of the jungle cry? (*Cries.*) Lions shouldn't cry.

John: Tell me what happened, and maybe I could help.

Lion: Do you know what today is?

John: Tuesday?

Lion: No. Today is the day they elected the king of the jungle. And I lost. (*Cries.*)

John: Do you know why you lost?

Lion: I don't know. I just did things kings are supposed to do.

John: Like what?

Lion: Well, I heard the antelopes were talking about me, so I made them wear muzzles on their mouths for a week.

John: That's terrible.

Lion: And the other week the elephants tore up my flower bed, so I made them haul logs all day with mud stuck up in their trunk.

John: That's awful.

Lion: But I had to. I'm the king of the jungle. Or at least I was.

John: But kings don't have to be mean.

Lion: They don't?

John: No. A king can be firm without being mean. If someone over you was mean, would you vote for him?

Lion: Well, no.

John: See! That's why the other animals didn't vote for you.

Lion: You mean that if I had been nice, they might have reelected me as their king?

John: That's right.

Lion: Oh, I wish I had it to do over again. I'd be nice this time.

Frog (*Enters running.*) Hey, Mr. Lion. Mr. Rabbit can't be king. So we were wondering if you'd still like to be king of the jungle.

Lion: Really? I'd love to. Let's go. (*To* **John**.) Hey, thanks for telling me what a king is really like. (*To* **Frog**.) You know, I've been noticing that lily pad you've been sitting on. It's worn out, and I think you deserve a new one.

Frog: Hey, that'd be great. (**Frog** *and* **Lion** *exit*.)

Narrator: So John said . . .

John: Wow!

Narrator: For he had helped the king of the jungle find out what it really meant to be a king. (*They exit.*)

Why Are People Different Colors?

by Louise Ulmer

Puppet: You know something? I've noticed that puppets and people come in different colors. Why is that? Wouldn't it be less confusing if everyone was all the same color?

Puppeteer: Before I answer that, can I ask you a question first? What did you plant in your garden last year?

Puppet: That's easy. I always plant daisies so I can tell if my boyfriend loves me or not. You know, love-me—love-me-not . . .

Puppeteer: Is that all?

Puppet: No, there's lots more. I had roses too. Red roses, and pink roses, and yellow . . .

Puppeteer: Any tulips?

Puppet: Yes, all colors. Red, purple, orange, every color you can think of.

Puppeteer: OK. Why did you plant so many colors?

Puppet: Is this a trick question?

Puppeteer: No, I'm serious.

Puppet: The answer is oblivious.

Puppeteer: I think you mean obvious. "Oblivious" means forgetful. "Obvious" means easy to understand.

Puppet: Oh, I get it. I'm obvious. You're oblivious.

Puppeteer: Come on now. You're right. The answer is obvious. You plant all different colors because you like them, don't you?

Puppet: I really do. I love all the colors of the rainbow. Is that why God made people different colors? Because he likes all different colors?

Puppeteer: I think so. Just look at all the colors in nature.

Puppet: Yeah, look at the flowers; look at the birds; look at the mud . . .

Puppeteer: The mud?

Puppet: Sure, even mud come in living colors.

Puppeteer: Yes, well, I hadn't thought about it before.

Puppet: Well, think about it. There's black mud, and brown mud, and red mud, and yellowish mud, and green mud.

Puppeteer: Green mud?

Puppet: I just threw that in to see if you were paying attention.

Puppeteer: Of course I am. You have my undivided attention. And I see what you mean. Mud is colorful.

Puppet: So why shouldn't people come in colors too?

Puppeteer: "Red and yellow, black and white,
They are precious in His sight."

Puppet: Those aren't the only colors people come in, you know?

Puppeteer: They aren't?

Puppet: No. There's brown. Light brown and dark brown. And you forgot pink.

Puppeteer: That's right. Babies are especially pink, aren't they?

Puppet: And some people are polka-dotted.

Puppeteer: Polka-dotted?

Puppet: Yeah. White with brown polka dots. You're kinda polka-dotted yourself.

Puppeteer: Those aren't polka dots. Those are freckles.

Puppet: They look like polks dots to me. But don't let it bother you. Lots of people are polka-dotted. Listen to the new verse I made up.

Jesus loves the little children,
All the children of the world.
Brown and pink and polka-dot,
Jesus loves them all a lot.
Jesus loves the little children of the world.

Isn't that good?

Puppeteer: Yes, it is. You know, I bet America is more like a garden than any other country in the world.

Puppet: Why, because a lot of people have gone to seed?

Puppeteer: No. Because there are so many different colors of people in this country.

Puppet: Yeah. And they're all beautiful. "Everybody's beautiful in his own way." Is that why they call it America the Beautiful?

Puppeteer: I bet it is.

Puppet: There's another reason.

Puppeteer: There is?

Puppet: Yeah. It sounds better than America the Gorgeous. Or America the Stunning. Or America the Ravishing.

Puppeteer: Come on. We better go. You're getting obnoxious.

Puppet: That's oblivious.

Puppeteer: No. I mean obnoxious.

Puppet: Tell me what that means.

Puppeteer: It should be obvious.

Puppet: I'm ready to go now. Wait. May I sing one more verse?

Puppeteer: Just one.

Puppet: OK. Jesus loves the little puppets,
All the puppets of the world.
Red and yellow, black and white.
They are precious in His sight.
Jesus loves the little puppets of the world.

Keeping God's World Beautiful

by Danny E. Bush

(Props: 2 trees, some cans, matches, paper, a ranger hat.)

Minnie (Enters humming, "God's Beautiful World"):
What a beautiful day!
What a beautiful world!
God's world is beautiful. I hope it will stay this way.
(She sits under a tree and begins to sing.)

"God's beautiful world, God's beautiful world.
I love God's beautiful world.
He made it for you. He made it for me.
I love God's beautiful world."

Milton and Mark (Enter throwing cans, paper and matches on the ground):

Milton: Man, what a great day this is!

Mark: Yeah, this sure is a nice park.

Milton: Want to go fishing?

Mark: OK, but let's just walk around for a while in this fresh air.

Minnie: Milton! What in the world are you and Mark doing?

Milton: Oh, hi, Minnie. We're just messing around.

Mark: Yeah, just messing around.

Minnie: Messing around is right! Just look at all the stuff you two have thrown on the ground! What a mess!

Milton: Listen to my sister, Mark. Gripe, gripe!

Mark: Yeah, gripe, gripe.

Milton: You'd think we were criminals or something.

Mark: Yeah, criminals or something.

Milton: Who cares? We haven't thrown all that much down.

Minnie: You and Mark haven't put much down? Why, just look at all that mess!

Milton: We didn't put all that stuff down. Somebody else must have put down a lot more than we did.

Mark: Yeah, a lot more than we did.

Minnie: A lot more than we did. Mark, you sound like an echo.

Mark: Yeah, like an echo, echo, echo, echo.

Milton: Yeah, like an echo, echo, echo, echo.

(**Milton** and **Mark** laugh.)

Minnie: It isn't funny! You two are just *some* of the people making a mess. But all you people put together can make a big mess.

Milton: You're really serious about this, aren't you, Minnie?

Minnie: Yes, I am, and you and Mark should get serious about it too. Mark, who made this beautiful world?

Mark: Well, the Bible says God did.

Minnie: Right. Then really we are just guests on God's good earth.

Milton: I think I'm beginning to see what you're getting at, Minnie. As guests we should act like guests. Right?

Minnie: Right!

Mark: Can I echo that?

Milton: You sure can.

Mark: We should act like guests.

Minnie: That's right. We should act like guests. Guests try to take care of things rather than mess up things.

(**Matt** comes walking along wearing a Ranger hat.)

Matt: Where are they? Where are they?

Milton: Where is who?

Matt: The people who keep messing up things around here.

Mark: Uh oh!

Minnie: Uh oh is right!

Milton: Minnie, you be quiet or we'll get in trouble.

Mark: Yeah, get in trouble.

Matt: Trouble. Who's in trouble?

Minnie: Oh, nobody in particular.

Milton: Whew, I hope not!

Mark: Whew, I hope not!

Matt: Does he do that much?

Minnie: What?

Matt: Make like an echo?

Minnie: Yes, but he's really a nice guy.

Matt: Fine. We need some more nice guys around here. Nice enough to not make a mess.

Minnie: See, what did I tell you two?

Matt: Two what?

Milton: Oh, nothing. We were just talking about the mess around here and how we are to be good guests on this earth.

Matt: Guests. That's a good idea.

Mark: We thought so.

Matt: Guests don't want to mess up something that doesn't belong to them.

Minnie: That's what "we" thought. God made this beautiful world and left us to take care of it. Some of "us" hadn't thought of that before.

Matt: It looks like a lot of people hadn't thought of it before. Thousands of dollars are spent each year in cleaning up the messes people make. Even more thousands of dollars are lost in forest fires. I wish more people would begin thinking of themselves as guests. It sure would make my job more easy.

Milton: Thousands of dollars each year?

Matt: Yes, thousands!

Mark: I guess we all better start getting serious about all this.

Minnie: We really should. I know a pretty song about God's beautiful world.

Milton: Hey, that's great! Please teach us the song, Minnie.

Mark: Yeah, please teach us the song, Minnie.

Matt: Yes, please teach us the song, Minnie. Now he's got me sounding like an echo!

(**Milton**, **Mark**, **Matt** and **Minnie** sing "God's Beautiful World" as they exit.)

Leader: In the Bible there is a beautiful Psalm written by David. It is Psalm 24, verse 1: "The earth is the Lord's, and the fulness thereof; the world, and they that dwell therein." God did make this beautiful world, and he made each one of us. God loves his world and you. Let's show our love to him by being good guests on his earth. Help keep this world beautiful.

Hi, God!

by Marianne Hawkins

(One puppet enters, bows head.)

Hi, God, how are you today? I just wanted to tell you that I really love you, God.

You know, God, I was outside a while ago, and I just wondered, does anybody ever thank you for the beautiful world that you made for us? God, the flowers are so pretty and the grass is soft and green. I sure don't think the world would be a very pretty place if you didn't make it that way. And God, how did you ever get the sky to be that blue? Anyway, thanks for giving us such a pretty world. Help people to take better care of it.

God, I'm sorry for the mean things I said to my friends at the baseball game. Help me to be nice and kind. I'm not happy when everybody's mad. God, help us to be good when we play together. I love my friends, God, and thank you for giving them to me.

God, my mama has been working awfully hard this week. Could you please help her get some rest today? And God, show me some ways that I can help her so she won't get so tired anymore.

Thank you for giving me a mama and a daddy who love me and take care of me. I love them a whole lot, God. Almost as much as I love *you*!

Oh God, I almost forgot . . . thanks for the things I learned at church today. Thank you for my Sunday School teacher (*or other leader*). I like to sing those songs about Jesus, and I like to hear the stories and Bible verses, too. You must really love us a lot, God, because you sent Jesus to die for us on the cross. Thanks, God, for all the things you've done to show how much you love me.

God, I gotta go now. Thanks for all the ways you take care of me. Well, I'll talk to you later, God. I love you, God. Amen.

(Puppet raises head, exits.)

Section V

FUN AND FELLOWSHIP

A Bible Lesson from the School of Hard Knocks

by Tom deGraaf

Narrator: The pastor has asked me to call attention to the fact that during the past few Sunday morning sermons, a couple of you have been nodding off to sleep. Now, granted, Sunday is a day of rest. However, both the pastor and I do feel that snoring aloud, while acceptable in some church council meetings, is nonconducive and, indeed, detrimental to the worship service proper. Therefore, the following true story is offered as evidence to the fact that a certain misfortune may await the Sunday service sleeper. Our story is entitled, "A Bible Lesson from the School of Hard Knocks," or "Sleeping in Church May Raise a Knot on Your Head."

(**Willie** *and* **Cool Charlie** *enter with Bibles, pretend that they are taking a seat in church, look toward audience as if pulpit is out there.*)

Willie (*Whispers, out of breath*): Whew! We made it, Cool Charlie! And just in the nick o' time.

Cool: Yeah. Man, that dash to the corner market and back between Sunday School and church is gettin' tougher and tougher to make. We must be gettin' old, Willie.

Willie: Yeah. It seemed a lot easier last year when we were only eleven. Oh oh. I think one of the deacons is going to make the announcements.

Deacon (*Offstage*): Good morning, everyone. We're happy to have you here at _____ Church. Here are the announcements and prayer requests for this morning as written in your bulletins.

Cool (*Whispers to* **Willie**): I just love this guy . . .

Deacon: Let's see. There will be a special called business meeting Wednesday night to discuss possible changes in our visitation card canvasing procedures. It seems that someone with a sense of humor has turned in several visitation cards with fictitious addresses; and last Tuesday, three couples inadvertently paid a call at the City Zoo. The meeting is at 7:30. Pot-luck supper to follow.

Willie: I can't wait to be a grown-up!

Deacon: On a more serious note . . . A dog exploded today in the Youth Department. There were no deaths; however, twelve were overcome by fur. It seems the kids were working on a living version of the Noah's Ark story when the accident occurred. Let's all remember to remember them all in prayer. And now here's Brother Pastor with the morning's sermon entitled, "Message from Brother _____."

Willie (*Whispers*): He uses that same title a lot. Oh, I think I feel a nap comin' over me, Cool Charlie.

Cool: Well, this is supposed to be a day of rest, right?

Willie: Right! (*They tilt their heads back. Their mouths drop open; they start to snore. Their heads start weaving.*)

Pastor (*Offstage*): Hey! Back there, you boys! Wake up!

Willie (*He and* **Charlie** *bang heads and wake up*): Ouch!

Pastor: Brother Weekers! Would you please attend to your son and Cool Charlie so I can continue my sermon?

Dad (*Enters beside boys, who are looking straight ahead, shaking*): Come on, Willie! You too, Cool Charlie. (*They follow* **Dad** *off, heads down in shame. In a moment they reappear, as if in another room.*) That was real thoughtful . . .

Willie (*Pleading*): Oh, we're sorry, Dad! Me and Cool Charlie are really sorry for falling asleep in church! Aren't we sorry, Cool Charlie?

Cool: Yeah, Mr. Weekers. We're sorry. It wasn't cool.

Dad: Well, boys, I'm a little disappointed . . . (*Pauses.*)

Willie: Aw, nuts, Dad! Say anything but that. I mean, give me a spankin' or somethin', but don't say that!

Cool: I feel like a real champ; I mean, it's bad enough that we was snorin', but to bump heads with a nerd like Willie . . . Aaayyeee . . . That ain't cool.

Dad: It could have been worse, boys. Much worse . . .

Willie: What do you mean, "It could have been worse"? I was humiliated when the pastor stopped his sermon on account of me and Cool Charlie sleepin'!

Dad: Yes, son, but I know of one young man who actully fell out a window and died.

Willie: He died during a sermon?

Cool: Hey, what do you mean, a guy died during a sermon?

Dad: Just what I said. Don't you guys know the story of the boy who fell out a third-story church window during a sermon?

Cool: Far out, Mr. Weekers! That reminds me of my nitwit cousin Philbert who broke his neck raking leaves.

Willie: He broke his neck rakin' leaves? How'd that happen?

Cool: He fell out of the tree . . . But never mind that nerd; I wanna hear your dad's story.

Dad: There's actually not much to it, but it does point out a possible problem for the rest of us who sleep in church. It seems that in Acts 20, Paul had come to preach at his friend's church in Troas. As it turned out, his friend didn't have a church building, so they all met up in a third-floor room for dinner and a sermon. Well, Paul got wound up in his sermon and preached and preached for hours and hours. It was actually the longest single sermon that anyone is history had ever preached up to that time.

Willie: Uh . . . how long was Paul's sermon?

Cool: Yeah, Mr. Weekers, how long was it?

Dad: Well . . . It was so long that three times Paul had to use a jumper cable on his tongue. (*Boys look at each other, shrug.*)

Dad: Anyway, it seems that one young lad went to sleep on a window ledge and fell out.

Willie: He fell three stories?

Dad: Yes, son. And the sudden stop at the street killed him. But Paul came down and miraculously brought the boy back to life!

Cool: Hey! Now that's what I call a real nice favor, Mr. Weekers.

Dad: Yes, it was, Cool Charlie. But I've known enough preachers to suspect that Paul mostly did it so he could continue his sermon. The point to remember, boys, is that sleeping in church is wrong and can get you into all kinds of trouble.

Willie: You're right, Dad. And from now on, me and Cool Charlie will never do it again!

Cool: Right, Mr. Weekers! No matter how tired and sleepy we might be, we won't let it get the best of us. Hey, Willie, what say you and me go apologize, like a couple of men, to Brother _____?

Willie: Good idea. Thanks for the story and advice, Dad. (*They exit.*)

Dad (*To audience*): They're not really bad boys. They just aren't quite old enough to enjoy and benefit from the music and sermon just yet, so they still fidgit or sleep. But that doesn't excuse the rest of you from Sunday siestas. No sirreee! So for those of us who still can't seem to stay awake, let me recommend an old tried and true method for attaining acute mental alertness. I've seen Brother _____ do it many times on his way to work or wherever. For exactly one-half hour, he straps his head to the exhaust fan of a fish restaurant. He says it keeps him wide awake for the next twenty-four hours or until his wife mentions taking out the garbage. I hope you've enjoyed our little lesson on sleeping in church! (*Exits.*)

Incident During a Visitation Campaign

by Tom deGraaf

Narrator: Visitation is a most important aspect of our church life and program here at _____. Each week many of our people faithfully dedicate an entire evening in order to go out into the community and invite people to our services. However, there are times when even the best of intentions and visitation techniques are stymied by large dogs, large doors, and small children.

The following story entitled "Incident During a Visitation Campaign" is a reenactment of Brother (Pastor's) first visit as a new pastor, many long years ago! The part of Brother (Pastor) will be played by our own Mr. Weekers, and the part of the little girl will be played by Sally. So, ladies and gentlemen, here's "Incident During a Visitation Campaign."

Dad (*Enters carrying visitation card*): Whew . . . finally . . . the last visitation card address. I can't believe I've visited thirty-eight places today . . . I've just got to get a car. Oh, well, let's see here. (*Looks at card.*) 809 is the house number. Here it is. The Thompsons' residence. It says here on the prospect card that there's a mother, father, and six children, all young. Well, here goes . . . (*Knocks on door.*)

    Sally (*Enters, pantomimes opening door, stands, looks at* **Dad** *silently.*)

Dad: Well, hello there, little girl. (*Pats her head.*)

Sal (*Very young, innocent*): Who are you?

Dad: I'm the pastor of the church you and your family visited last Sunday.

Sally: What do you want today, Mr. Preacher? More money?

Dad: Uh, no, honey. That was called an offering. Are your mommy and daddy home? I'd like to see them.

Sal (*Sweetly*): Well, you can't!

Dad (*Pauses*): Will you call them to the door, dear?

Sal (*Sweetly*): No.

Dad (*Exasperated*): Why not?

Sally: Mommy's not home. She went to the hospital this morning to have another baby sister.

Dad: Oh, my . . .

Sally: And Daddy's asleep on the couch. I don't wake him up or he will yell at me. Mommy says he's like a bear when he gets woken up!

Dad: You have a big brother, don't you? Where is he?

Sally: In the kitchen. He's five. He is making a chocolate cake to surprise Daddy.

Dad: I'm sure he'll be surprised. Where are your sisters?

Sally: Kelly is upstairs taking a big, big, big bubble bath. Susie is in the living room changing the dirt in her ant farm.

Dad (*Looks at card*): Who's watching the baby?

Sally: I am! I'm a big girl—almost four!

Dad: Uh, don't you think you'd better go and check on him?

Sally: OK. I'll be right back.

Dad (*To himself*): I can just imagine what that house must look like with six children turned loose, chocolate cake batter, bubbles, ant farm dirt . . . Wait till their dad wakes up . . .

Sally (*Reenters*): Jon-Jon was playing in the kitchen sink. He pushed the hamster down the disposal, but I got the kitty away from him. I think we knocked down the curtains . . . (*Looks behind her.*) Is that soapy water coming down the stairs? I think my sister made too big of a bubble bath. Do you think I should wake Daddy?

Dad (*Looks blankly at the audience, then back at* **Sally**): Yes, I think maybe you should wake up your daddy, but I think I'll leave before you do. Bye, honey. It's been a long day. (*Exits quickly.*)

Sally: Byeee, Mr. Preacher! (*Exits.*) Daddy! Daddy! Time to wake up!